THE

LAY

OF

THE LAST MINSTREL

—

A POEM IN SIX CANTOS

THE

LAY

OF

THE LAST MINSTREL

A POEM IN SIX CANTOS

BY

WALTER SCOTT

INTRODUCTION BY

THE DUKE OF BUCCLEUCH

BOWHILL
EDITION

Published in 2013 by
Birlinn Limited

BIRLINN

West Newington House
10 Newington Road
Edinburgh
EH9 1QS

www.birlinn.co.uk

This edition taken from the eighth edition (1808) printed for
Longman, Hurst, Rees and Orme, London and
A. Constable and Co., Edinburgh

Introduction copyright © the Duke of Buccleuch 2013

ISBN: 978 1 78027 185 9

British Library Cataloguing-in-Publication Data
A catalogue record for this book is available from the British Library

Typeset by Iolaire Typesetting, Newtonmore
Printed and bound by Grafica Veneta
www.graficaveneta.com

INTRODUCTION

TO THE

BOWHILL EDITION

BY

THE DUKE OF BUCCLEUCH

The much loved Dame Jean Maxwell Scott, the last of Sir Walter Scott's direct descendants to live at Abbotsford, was my wife's godmother. Shortly after we were married some thirty years ago she gave her a special copy of *The Lay of the Last Minstrel* which came, as she wrote, from the author's great-great-great-granddaughter to the new Countess of Dalkeith, successor to the title once held by Scott's friend and enthusiastic muse, Harriet. Already on its eighth print run in 1808, it is this copy which Birlinn has faithfully transcribed as the basis for the new Bowhill edition of *The Lay of the Last Minstrel.*

That the first edition had appeared just three years before in January 1805 was testament to the phenomenal success of Scott's first long narrative poem. His *Minstrelsy of the Scottish Border,* the compendium of the mainly oral verse of the region, had earned him wide respect. The *Lay* paved the path to his financial fortune. Sales exceeded 18,000 in five years, an astonishing figure at the time and although the bargain he struck with his publishers was so unbalanced that they embarrassedly made it up to him with the purchase of a fine horse, he was able to command an advance of 1,000 guineas (£1,050) for his next work, *Marmion.*

The Minstrel's tale is set in the sixteenth century but Scott has him tell it at the end of the seventeenth century on a stormy night in gaunt Newark tower in the Yarrow valley to the widowed Anna, Duchess of Buccleuch, who 'though born in such a high degree . . . had wept o'er Monmouth's bloody tomb'.

Place and family names of the Scottish and English borders
abound. Centred on Branxholme, the old Scott family fortress
near Hawick, it is a complex tale of romance and revenge, of
noble motives and base methods including sorcery, petty feuding
and high politics. Presiding over events is an earlier Buccleuch
widow, in the poem just called the Ladye, whose husband, Sir
Walter, had fallen in a bitter feud with, amongst others, a Lord
Cranstoun, who unfortunately has become the great love of
her daughter, Lady Margaret. In her determination to thwart
the romance, the old lady deploys the loyal and chivalrous Sir
William of Deloraine, whose despatch to retrieve the magic book
of wizard Michael Scott from his tomb in Melrose Abbey at dead
of night provides some of the poem's most vivid images. A series
of disasters, including loss of the book and kidnapping of the
young Buccleuch heir, follows, mainly due to the intervention of
the Goblin Page, a magically endowed and malicious dwarf figure
attached to Cranstoun. Even Scott acknowledged later that he
might be 'an excrescence', but the character had been urged on
him by Harriet, Countess of Dalkeith – his 'lovely chieftainess
. . . who has more of the angel in face and temper than anyone
alive' – who was a powerful influence in encouraging him to
write the poem. Eventually after great forces have been deployed,
an English army led by Lords Dacre and Howard, and all the
Border clans aroused, it climaxes in mortal combat between
Cranstoun disguised as Deloraine and the English champion,
Sir Richard Musgrave, who, to general lamenting, ends up as the
only real casualty of all six cantos.

Yet for all the often fantastical complexities the poem is a
galloping tale. Completed, Scott later claimed, 'about the rate
of a canto a week', he described it to a friend as 'a light horse-
man sort of stanza'. Its irregular metre was strikingly original to
contemporary readers as well as providing room for manoeuvre
for the writer. Even at the time there was some controversy
in literary circles as to the extent Scott had been inspired by

having heard a recitation of Coleridge's 'Christabel', but Coleridge himself was generous and it was as much the scope of the narrative tale that enthralled readers as the verse. That was notwithstanding the prominence given to Scott's (and this writer's) own family and its historic glory amongst the Border clans in what John Sutherland vividly describes as 'less a poem than a totem pole in verse'.

The *Lay*'s popularity rested not just on the number of copies shifted but also on a spread of critical enthusiasm, starting with Wordsworth who wrote that 'the novelty of the manners, the clear picturesque descriptions, and the easy glowing energy of much of the verse, greatly delight me'. Its appeal spanned the political divide, admired as much by Charles James Fox as by William Pitt, the Prime Minister, who described it as the sort of thing 'which I might have expected in painting but could never have fancied capable of being given in poetry'.

I hope that with this publication its appeal might once again span the centuries. There are sections, as happens with Scott, which even the most devoted reader will skip by. There are lines – 'Breathes there the man, with soul so dead' or 'O Caledonia! stern and wild' – that are almost too familiar. But overall it is a tale of wonderful drama, vividly told, full of great descriptive poetry – 'the gay beams of lightsome day/Gild, but to flout, the ruins grey' of Melrose Abbey – and above all passages of beauty, true love is 'the secret sympathy, The silver link, the silken tie/ Which heart to heart, and mind to mind, In body and in soul can bind'. Beneath all the hurly burly and fun Scott's humanity, the foundation of all his writing, is there, and it is timeless.

Richard Buccleuch

THE

LAY

OF

THE LAST MINSTREL,

A POEM;

THE EIGHTH EDITION.

WITH

BALLADS AND LYRICAL PIECES.

BY

WALTER SCOTT, Esq.

Dum relego, scripsisse pudet, quia plurima cerno,
Me quoque, qui feci, judice, digna lini.

LONDON :

PRINTED FOR LONGMAN, HURST, REES, AND ORME,
PATERNOSTER-ROW, AND A. CONSTABLE AND CO. EDINBURGH ;
BY JAMES BALLANTYNE AND CO. EDINBURGH.

1808.

THE

LAY

OF

THE LAST MINSTREL

CANTO FIRST

INTRODUCTION

—

THE way was long, the wind was cold,
The Minstrel was infirm and old;
His withered cheek, and tresses gray,
Seemed to have known a better day;
The harp, his sole remaining joy,
Was carried by an orphan boy;
The last of all the bards was he,
Who sung of Border chivalry.
For, well-a-day! their date was fled,
His tuneful brethren all were dead;
And he, neglected and oppressed,
Wished to be with them, and at rest.
No more, on prancing palfrey borne,
He carolled, light as lark at morn;
No longer courted and caressed,
High placed in hall, a welcome guest,
He poured to lord and lady gay,
The unpremeditated lay:
Old times were changed, old manners gone;
A stranger filled the Stuart's throne;
The bigots of the iron time
Had called his harmless art a crime.

A wandering Harper, scorned and poor,
He begged his bread from door to door;
And tuned, to please a peasant's ear,
The harp, a king had loved to hear.

He passed where Newark's stately tower
Looks out from Yarrow's birchen bower:
The Minstrel gazed with wishful eye—
No humbler resting-place was nigh.
With hesitating step, at last,
The embattled portal-arch he passed,
Whose ponderous grate and massy bar
Had oft rolled back the tide of war,
But never closed the iron door
Against the desolate and poor.
The Duchess* marked his weary pace,
His timid mien, and reverend face,
And bade her page the menials tell,
That they should tend the old man well:
For she had known adversity,
Though born in such a high degree;
In pride of power, in beauty's bloom,
Had wept o'er Monmouth's bloody tomb!

When kindness had his wants supplied,
And the old man was gratified,
Began to rise his minstrel pride:

---

* Anne, Duchess of Buccleuch and Monmouth, representative of the ancient
Lords of Buccleuch, and widow of the unfortunate James, Duke of Monmouth, who
was beheaded in 1685.

And he began to talk anon,
Of good Earl Francis,* dead and gone,
And of Earl Walter,† rest him God;
A braver ne'er to battle rode:
And how full many a tale he knew,
Of the old warriors of Buccleuch;
And, would the noble Duchess deign
To listen to an old man's strain,
Though stiff his hand, his voice though weak,
He thought even yet, the sooth to speak,
That, if she loved the harp to hear,
He could make music to her ear.

The humble boon was soon obtained;
The Aged Minstrel audience gained.
But, when he reached the room of state,
Where she, with all her ladies, sate,
Perchance he wished his boon denied;
For, when to tune his harp he tried,
His trembling hand had lost the ease,
Which marks security to please;
And scenes, long past, of joy and pain,
Came wildering o'er his aged brain—
He tried to tune his harp in vain.
The pitying Duchess praised its chime,
And gave him heart, and gave him time,
Till every string's according glee
Was blended into harmony.

* Francis Scot, Earl of Buccleuch, father of the Duchess.
† Walter, Earl of Buccleuch, grandfather of the Duchess, and a celebrated warrior.

And then, he said, he would full fain
He could recal an ancient strain,
He never thought to sing again.
It was not framed for village churles,
But for high dames and mighty earls:
He had played it to King Charles the Good,
When he kept court in Holyrood;
And much he wished, yet feared, to try
The long-forgotten melody.

Amid the strings his fingers strayed,
And an uncertain warbling made,
And oft he shook his hoary head.
But when he caught the measure wild,
The old man raised his face, and smiled;
And lightened up his faded eye
With all a poet's extacy!
In varying cadence, soft or strong,
He swept the sounding chords along:
The present scene, the future lot,
His toils, his wants, were all forgot;
Cold diffidence, and age's frost,
In the full tide of song were lost;
Each blank, in faithless memory void,
The poet's glowing thought supplied;
And, while his harp responsive rung,
'Twas thus the LATEST MINSTREL sung.

THE

LAY OF THE LAST MINSTREL

CANTO FIRST

I

THE feast was over in Branksome tower,
And the Ladye had gone to her secret bower;
Her bower, that was guarded by word and by spell,
Deadly to hear, and deadly to tell—
Jesu Maria, shield us well!
No living wight, save the Ladye alone,
Had dared to cross the threshold stone.

II

The tables were drawn, it was idlesse all;
    Knight, and page, and household squire,
Loitered through the lofty hall,
    Or crowded round the ample fire:
The stag-hounds, weary with the chace,
    Lay stretched upon the rushy floor,
And urged, in dreams, the forest race,
    From Teviot-stone to Eskdale-moor.

III

Nine-and-twenty knights of fame
   Hung their shields in Branksome Hall;
Nine-and-twenty squires of name
   Brought them their steeds from bower to stall;
Nine-and-twenty yeomen tall
   Waited, duteous, on them all:
They were all knights of mettle true,
   Kinsmen to the bold Buccleuch.

IV

Ten of them were sheathed in steel,
With belted sword, and spur on heel:
They quitted not their harness bright,
Neither by day, nor yet by night:
   They lay down to rest
   With corslet laced,
Pillowed on buckler cold and hard;
      They carved at the meal
      With gloves of steel,
And they drank the red wine through the helmet barred.

V

Ten squires, ten yeomen, mail-clad men,
Waited the beck of the warders ten;
Thirty steeds, both fleet and wight,
Stood saddled in stable day and night,
Barbed with frontlet of steel, I trow,
And with Jedwood-axe at saddle-bow;

A hundred more fed free in stall:—
Such was the custom of Branksome Hall.

VI

Why do these steeds stand ready dight?
Why watch these warriors, armed, by night?—
They watch, to hear the blood-hound baying;
They watch, to hear the war-horn braying;
To see St George's red cross streaming,
To see the midnight beacon gleaming;
   They watch, against Southern force and guile,
     Lest Scroop, or Howard, or Percy's powers,
     Threaten Branksome's lordly towers,
   From Warkworth, or Naworth, or merry Carlisle.

VII

Such is the custom of Branksome Hall.—
   Many a valiant knight is here;
But he, the Chieftain of them all,
His sword hangs rusting on the wall,
   Beside his broken spear.
Bards long shall tell,
How Lord Walter fell!
When startled burghers fled, afar,
The furies of the Border war;
When the streets of high Dunedin
Saw lances gleam, and falchions redden,
And heard the slogan's * deadly yell—
Then the Chief of Branksome fell.

---

* The war-cry, or gathering word, of a Border clan.

VIII

Can piety the discord heal,
　Or staunch the death-feud's enmity?
Can Christian lore, can patriot zeal,
　Can love of blessed charity?
No! vainly to each holy shrine,
　In mutual pilgrimage, they drew;
Implored, in vain, the grace divine
　For chiefs, their own red falchions slew:
While Cessford owns the rule of Car,
　While Ettrick boasts the line of Scott,
The slaughtered chiefs, the mortal jar,
The havoc of the feudal war,
　Shall never, never be forgot!

IX

In sorrow, o'er Lord Walter's bier
　The warlike foresters had bent;
And many a flower, and many a tear,
　Old Teviot's maids and matrons lent:
But o'er her warrior's bloody bier
The Ladye dropped nor flower nor tear!
　Vengeance, deep-brooding o'er the slain,
　　Had locked the source of softer woe;
　And burning pride, and high disdain,
　　Forbade the rising tear to flow;
　Until, amid his sorrowing clan,
　　Her son lisped from the nurse's knee—
　　"And, if I live to be a man,
　　My father's death revenged shall be!"

Then fast the mother's tears did seek
To dew the infant's kindling cheek.

X

All loose her negligent attire,
    All loose her golden hair,
Hung Margaret o'er her slaughtered sire,
    And wept in wild despair.
But not alone the bitter tear
    Had filial grief supplied;
For hopeless love, and anxious fear,
    Had lent their mingled tide:
Nor in her mother's altered eye
Dared she to look for sympathy.
    Her lover, 'gainst her father's clan,
        With Car in arms had stood,
    When Mathouse-burn to Melrose ran,
        All purple with their blood;
And well she knew, her mother dread,
Before Lord Cranstoun she should wed,
Would see her on her dying bed.

XI

Of noble race the Ladye came;
    Her father was a clerk of fame,
    Of Bethune's line of Picardie:
He learned the art, that none may name,
    In Padua, far beyond the sea.
Men said, he changed his mortal frame

By feat of magic mystery;
For when, in studious mood, he paced
 St Andrew's cloistered hall,
His form no darkening shadow traced
 Upon the sunny wall!

XII

And of his skill, as bards avow,
 He taught that Ladye fair,
Till to her bidding she could bow
 The viewless forms of air.
And now she sits in secret bower,
In old Lord David's western tower,
And listens to a heavy sound,
That moans the mossy turrets round.
Is it the roar of Teviot's tide,
That chafes against the scaur's * red side?
Is it the wind, that swings the oaks?
Is it the echo from the rocks?
What may it be, the heavy sound,
That moans old Branksome's turrets round?

XIII

At the sullen, moaning sound,
 The ban-dogs bay and howl;
And, from the turrets round,
 Loud whoops the startled owl.

---

* *Scaur*, a precipitous bank of earth.

In the hall, both squire and knight
  Swore that a storm was near,
And looked forth to view the night;
  But the night was still and clear!

XIV

From the sound of Teviot's tide,
Chafing with the mountain's side,
From the groan of the wind-swung oak,
From the sullen echo of the rock,
From the voice of the coming storm,
    The Ladye knew it well!
It was the Spirit of the Flood that spoke,
  And he called on the Spirit of the Fell.

XV

RIVER SPIRIT

"Sleep'st thou, brother?"

MOUNTAIN SPIRIT

    — "Brother, nay—
On my hills the moon-beams play.
From Craik-cross to Skelfhill-pen,
By every rill, in every glen,
  Merry elves their morrice pacing,
    To aerial minstrels,
  Emerald rings on brown heath tracing,
    Trip it deft and merrily.
Up, and mark their nimble feet!
Up, and list their music sweet!"

XVI

RIVER SPIRIT

"Tears of an imprisoned maiden
    Mix with my polluted stream;
Margaret of Branksome, sorrow-laden,
    Mourns beneath the moon's pale beam.
Tell me, thou, who viewest the stars,
When shall cease these feudal jars?
What shall be the maiden's fate?
Who shall be the maiden's mate?"

XVII

MOUNTAIN SPIRIT

"Arthur's slow wain his course doth roll,
In utter darkness, round the pole;
The Northern Bear lowers black and grim;
Orion's studded belt is dim;
Twinkling faint, and distant far,
Shimmers through mist each planet star;
    Ill may I read their high decree:
But no kind influence deign they shower
On Teviot's tide and Branksome's tower,
    Till pride be quelled, and love be free."—

XVIII

The unearthly voices ceast,
    And the heavy sound was still;
It died on the river's breast,

It died on the side of the hill.—
But round Lord David's tower
   The sound still floated near;
For it rung in the Ladye's bower,
   And it rung in the Ladye's ear.
She raised her stately head,
   And her heart throbbed high with pride:—
"Your mountains shall bend,
And your streams ascend,
   Ere Margaret be our foeman's bride!"—

XIX

The Ladye sought the lofty hall,
   Where many a bold retainer lay,
And, with jocund din, among them all,
   Her son pursued his infant play.
A fancied moss-trooper, the boy
   The truncheon of a spear bestrode,
And round the hall, right merrily,
   In mimic foray * rode.
Even bearded knights, in arms grown old,
   Share in his frolic gambols bore,
Albeit their hearts, of rugged mould,
   Were stubborn as the steel they wore.
For the gray warriors prophesied,
   How the brave boy, in future war,
Should tame the Unicorn's pride,
   Exalt the Crescents and the Star. †

---

* *Foray*, a predatory inroad.
† Alluding to the armorial bearings of the Scotts and Cars.

XX

The Ladye forgot her purpose high,
    One moment, and no more;
One moment gazed with a mother's eye,
    As she paused at the arched door:
Then, from amid the armed train,
She called to her William of Deloraine.

XXI

A stark moss-trooping Scott was he,
As e'er couched Border lance by knee:
Through Solway sands, through Tarras moss,
Blindfold, he knew the paths to cross;
By wily turns, by desperate bounds,
Had baffled Percy's best blood-hounds;
In Eske, or Liddel, fords were none,
But he would ride them, one by one;
Alike to him was time or tide,
December's snow, or July's pride;
Alike to him was tide or time,
Moonless midnight, or matin prime:
Steady of heart, and stout of hand,
As ever drove prey from Cumberland;
Five times outlawed had he been,
By England's king, and Scotland's queen.

XXII

"Sir William of Deloraine, good at need,
Mount thee on the wightest steed;

Spare not to spur, nor stint to ride,
Until thou come to fair Tweedside;
And in Melrose's holy pile
Seek thou the Monk of St Mary's aisle.
   Greet the Father well from me;
      Say, that the fated hour is come,
   And to-night he shall watch with thee,
      To win the treasure of the tomb:
For this will be St Michael's night,
And, though stars be dim, the moon is bright;
And the Cross, of bloody red,
Will point to the grave of the mighty dead.

XXIII

"What he gives thee, see thou keep;
Stay not thou for food or sleep:
Be it scroll, or be it book,
Into it, knight, thou must not look;
If thou readest, thou art lorn!
Better had'st thou ne'er been born."

XXIV

   "O swiftly can speed my dapple-gray steed,
      Which drinks of the Teviot clear;
Ere break of day," the warrior 'gan say,
   "Again will I be here:

And safer by none may thy errand be done,
   Than, noble dame, by me;
Letter nor line know I never a one,
   Wer't my neck-verse at Hairibee." *

XXV

Soon in his saddle sate he fast,
And soon the steep descent he past,
Soon crossed the sounding barbican, †
And soon the Teviot side he won.
Eastward the wooded path he rode;
Green hazels o'er his basnet nod:
He passed the Peel ‡ of Goldiland,
And crossed old Borthwick's roaring strand;
Dimly he viewed the Moat-hill's mound,
Where Druid shades still flitted round:
In Hawick twinkled many a light;
Behind him soon they set in night;
And soon he spurred his courser keen
Beneath the tower of Hazeldean.

XXVI

The clattering hoofs the watchmen mark;—
"Stand, ho! thou courier of the dark."
"For Branksome, ho!" the knight rejoined,
And left the friendly tower behind.

---

*   *Hairibee*, the place of executing the Border marauders at Carlisle. The *neck-verse* is the beginning of the 51st psalm, *Miserere mei*, &c. anciently read by criminals claiming the benefit of clergy.

†   *Barbican*, the defence of the outer gate of a feudal castle.

‡   *Peel*, a Border tower.

He turned him now from Teviotside,
    And, guided by the tinkling rill,
Northward the dark ascent did ride,
    And gained the moor at Horseliehill;
Broad on the left before him lay,
For many a mile, the Roman way. *

XXVII

A moment now he slacked his speed,
A moment breathed his panting steed;
Drew saddle-girth and corslet-band,
And loosened in the sheath his brand.
On Minto-crags the moon-beams glint,
Where Barnhill hewed his bed of flint;
Who flung his outlawed limbs to rest,
Where falcons hang their giddy nest,
Mid cliffs, from whence his eagle-eye
For many a league his prey could spy;
Cliffs doubling, on their echoes borne,
The terrors of the robber's horn;
Cliffs, which, for many a later year,
The warbling Doric reed shall hear,
When some sad swain shall teach the grove,
Ambition is no cure for love.

XXVIII

Unchallenged, thence past Deloraine
To ancient Riddel's fair domain,

---

* An ancient Roman road, crossing through part of Roxburghshire.

Where Aill, from mountains freed,
Down from the lakes did raving come;
Each wave was crested with tawny foam,
    Like the mane of a chesnut steed.
In vain! no torrent, deep or broad,
Might bar the bold moss-trooper's road.

XXIX

At the first plunge the horse sunk low,
And the water broke o'er the saddle-bow;
Above the foaming tide, I ween,
Scarce half the charger's neck was seen;
For he was barded * from counter to tail,
And the rider was armed complete in mail;
Never heavier man and horse
Stemmed a midnight torrent's force.
The warrior's very plume, I say,
Was daggled by the dashing spray;
Yet, through good heart, and Our Ladye's grace,
At length he gained the landing place.

XXX

Now Bowden Moor the march-man won,
    And sternly shook his plumed head,
As glanced his eye o'er Halidon; †
    For on his soul the slaughter red

---

* *Barded*, or barbed, applied to a horse accoutered with defensive armour.
† *Halidon-hill*, on which the battle of Melrose was fought

Of that unhallowed morn arose,
When first the Scott and Car were foes;
When royal James beheld the fray,
Prize to the victor of the day;
When Home and Douglas, in the van,
Bore down Buccleuch's retiring clan,
Till gallant Cessford's heart-blood dear
Reeked on dark Elliot's Border spear.

XXXI

In bitter mood he spurred fast,
And soon the hated heath was past;
And far beneath, in lustre wan,
Old Melros' rose, and fair Tweed ran:
Like some tall rock, with lichens gray,
Seemed, dimly huge, the dark Abbaye.
When Hawick he passed, had curfew rung,
Now midnight lauds * were in Melrose sung.
The sound, upon the fitful gale,
In solemn wise did rise and fail,
Like that wild harp, whose magic tone
Is wakened by the winds alone.
But when Melrose he reached, 'twas silence all;
He meetly stabled his steed in stall,
And sought the convent's lonely wall.

---

* *Lauds*, the midnight service of the Catholic church.

HERE paused the harp; and, with its swell,
The Master's fire and courage fell:
Dejectedly, and low, he bowed,
And, gazing timid on the crowd,
He seemed to seek, in every eye,
If they approved his minstrelsy;
And, diffident of present praise,
Somewhat he spoke of former days,
And how old age, and wandering long,
Had done his hand and harp some wrong.

   The Duchess, and her daughters fair,
And every gentle ladye there,
Each after each, in due degree,
Gave praises to his melody;
His hand was true, his voice was clear,
And much they longed the rest to hear.
Encouraged thus, the Aged Man,
After meet rest, again began.

THE

LAY OF THE LAST MINSTREL

CANTO SECOND

I

If thou would'st view fair Melrose aright,
Go visit it by the pale moon-light;
For the gay beams of lightsome day
Gild, but to flout, the ruins gray.
When the broken arches are black in night,
And each shafted oriel glimmers white;
When the cold light's uncertain shower
Streams on the ruined central tower;
When buttress and buttress, alternately,
Seem framed of ebon and ivory;
When silver edges the imagery,
And the scrolls that teach thee to live and die;
When distant Tweed is heard to rave,
And the owlet to hoot o'er the dead man's grave,
Then go,—but go alone the while—
Then view St David's ruined pile;
And, home returning, soothly swear,
Was never scene so sad and fair!

II

Short halt did Deloraine make there;
Little recked he of the scene so fair.
With dagger's hilt, on the wicket strong,
He struck full loud, and struck full long.
The porter hurried to the gate—
"Who knocks so loud, and knocks so late?"—
"From Branksome I," the warrior cried;
And strait the wicket opened wide:
For Branksome's chiefs had in battle stood,
    To fence the rights of fair Melrose;
And lands and livings, many a rood,
    Had gifted the shrine for their souls' repose.

III

Bold Deloraine his errand said;
The porter bent his humble head;
With torch in hand, and feet unshod,
And noiseless step, the path he trod:
The arched cloisters, far and wide,
Rang to the warrior's clanking stride;
Till, stooping low his lofty crest,
He entered the cell of the ancient priest,
And lifted his barred aventayle, *
To hail the monk of St Mary's aisle.

* *Aventayle*, visor of the helmet.

IV

"The Ladye of Branksome greets thee by me;
   Says, that the fated hour is come,
And that to-night I shall watch with thee,
   To win the treasure of the tomb."—
From sackcloth couch the Monk arose,
   With toil his stiffened limbs he reared;
A hundred years had flung their snows
   On his thin locks and floating beard.

V

And strangely on the knight looked he,
   And his blue eyes gleamed wild and wide;—
"And, dar'st thou, warrior! seek to see
   What heaven and hell alike would hide?
My breast, in belt of iron pent,
   With shirt of hair and scourge of thorn;
For threescore years, in penance spent,
   My knees those flinty stones have worn;
Yet all too little to atone
For knowing what should ne'er be known.
Would'st thou thy every future year
   In ceaseless prayer and penance drie,
Yet wait thy latter end with fear—
   Then, daring warrior, follow me!"

VI

"Penance, father, will I none;
Prayer know I hardly one;

For mass or prayer can I rarely tarry,
Save to patter an Ave Mary,
When I ride on a Border foray:
Other prayer can I none;
So speed me my errand, and let me begone."—

VII

Again on the Knight looked the Churchman old,
　　And again he sighed heavily;
For he had himself been a warrior bold,
　　And fought in Spain and Italy.
And he thought on the days that were long since by,
When his limbs were strong, and his courage was
　　　　high:—
Now, slow and faint, he led the way,
　　Where, cloistered round, the garden lay;
　　The pillared arches were over their head,
And beneath their feet were the bones of the dead.

VIII

Spreading herbs, and flowrets bright,
Glistened with the dew of night;
Nor herb, nor flowret, glistened there,
But was carved in the cloister-arches as fair.
　　The Monk gazed long on the lovely moon,
　　　　Then into the night he looked forth;
　　And red and bright the streamers light
　　　　Were dancing in the glowing north.

So had he seen, in fair Castile,
    The youth in glittering squadrons start;
Sudden the flying jennet wheel,
    And hurl the unexpected dart.
He knew, by the streamers that shot so bright,
That spirits were riding the northern light.

IX

By a steel-clenched postern door,
    They entered now the chancel tall;
The darkened roof rose high aloof
    On pillars, lofty, and light, and small;
The key-stone, that locked each ribbed aisle,
Was a fleur-de-lys, or a quatre-feuille;
The corbells * were carved grotesque and grim;
And the pillars, with clustered shafts so trim,
With base and with capital flourished around,
Seemed bundles of lances which garlands had
      bound.

X

Full many a scutcheon and banner, riven,
Shook to the cold night-wind of heaven,
    Around the screened altar's pale;
And there the dying lamps did burn,
Before thy low and lonely urn,
O gallant Chief of Otterburne,

---

   * *Corbells*, the projections from which the arches spring, usually cut in a fantastic face, or mask.

And thine, dark Knight of Liddesdale!
O fading honours of the dead!
O high ambition, lowly laid!

XI

The moon on the east oriel shone,
Through slender shafts of shapely stone,
    By foliaged tracery combined;
Thou would'st have thought some fairy's hand,
'Twixt poplars straight the ozier wand,
    In many a freakish knot, had twined;
Then framed a spell, when the work was done,
And changed the willow wreaths to stone.
    The silver light, so pale and faint,
    Shewed many a prophet, and many a saint,
       Whose image on the glass was dyed;
    Full in the midst, his Cross of Red
    Triumphant Michael brandished,
       And trampled the Apostate's pride.
The moon-beam kissed the holy pane,
And threw on the pavement a bloody stain.

XII

They sate them down on a marble stone,
    A Scottish monarch slept below;
Thus spoke the Monk, in solemn tone:—
    "I was not always a man of woe:
For Paynim countries I have trod,
And fought beneath the Cross of God;

Now, strange to my eyes thine arms appear,
And their iron clang sounds strange to my ear.

XIII

"In these far climes, it was my lot
To meet the wondrous Michael Scott;
 A wizard of such dreaded fame,
That when, in Salamanca's cave,
Him listed his magic wand to wave,
 The bells would ring in Notre Dame!
Some of his skill he taught to me;
And, Warrior, I could say to thee
The words, that cleft Eildon hills in three.
 And bridled the Tweed with a curb of stone:
But to speak them were a deadly sin;
And for having but thought them my heart within,
 A treble penance must be done.

XIV

"When Michael lay on his dying bed,
His conscience was awakened;
He bethought him of his sinful deed,
And he gave me a sign to come with speed:
I was in Spain when the morning rose,
But I stood by his bed ere evening close.
The words may not again be said,
That he spoke to me, on death-bed laid;
They would rend this Abbaye's massy nave,
And pile it in heaps above his grave.

XV

"I swore to bury his Mighty Book,
That never mortal might therein look;
And never to tell where it was hid,
Save at his chief of Branksome's need;
And when that need was past and o'er,
Again the volume to restore.
I buried him on St Michael's night,
When the bell tolled one, and the moon was bright;
And I dug his chamber among the dead,
When the floor of the chancel was stained red,
That his patron's Cross might over him wave,
And scare the fiends from the Wizard's grave.

XVI

"It was a night of woe and dread,
When Michael in the tomb I laid!
Strange sounds along the chancel past,
The banners waved without a blast,"—
—Still spoke the Monk, when the bell tolled
        one!—
I tell you, that a braver man
Than William of Deloraine, good at need,
Against a foe ne'er spurred a steed;
Yet somewhat was he chilled with dread,
And his hair did bristle upon his head.

XVII

"Lo, Warrior! now, the Cross of Red
Points to the grave of the mighty dead.

Within it burns a wondrous light,
To chase the spirits that love the night;
That lamp shall burn unquenchably,
Until the eternal doom shall be."—
Slow moved the Monk to the broad flag-stone,
Which the bloody Cross was traced upon:
He pointed to a secret nook;
An iron bar the warrior took;
And the Monk made a sign with his withered
    hand,
The grave's huge portal to expand.

XVIII

With beating heart to the task he went;
His sinewy frame o'er the grave-stone bent;
With bar of iron heaved amain,
Till the toil-drops fell from his brows, like rain.
It was by dint of passing strength,
That he moved the massy stone at length.
I would you had been there, to see
How the light broke forth so gloriously,
Streamed upward to the chancel roof,
And through the galleries far aloof!
No earthly flame blazed e'er so bright:
It shone like heaven's own blessed light,
    And, issuing from the tomb,
Shewed the Monk's cowl, and visage pale,
Danced on the dark-brow'd Warrior's mail,
    And kissed his waving plume.

XIX

Before their eyes the Wizard lay,
As if he had not been dead a day.
His hoary beard in silver rolled,
He seemed some seventy winters old;
 A palmer's amice wrapped him round,
 With a wrought Spanish baldric bound,
  Like a pilgrim from beyond the sea:
 His left hand held his Book of Might;
 A silver cross was in his right;
  The lamp was placed beside his knee:
High and majestic was his look,
At which the fellest fiends had shook,
And all unruffled was his face:—
They trusted his soul had gotten grace.

XX

Often had William of Deloraine
Rode through the battle's bloody plain,
And trampled down the warriors slain,
 And neither known remorse or awe;
Yet now remorse and awe he own'd;
His breath came thick, his head swam round,
 When this strange scene of death he saw.
Bewildered and unnerved he stood,
And the priest prayed fervently, and loud:
With eyes averted prayed he;
He might not endure the sight to see,
Of the man he had loved so brotherly.

XXI

And when the priest his death-prayer had prayed,
Thus unto Deloraine he said:—
"Now, speed thee what thou hast to do,
Or, Warrior, we may dearly rue;
For those, thou mayest not look upon,
Are gathering fast round the yawning stone!"
Then Deloraine, in terror, took
From the cold hand the Mighty Book,
With iron clasped, and with iron bound:—
He thought, as he took it, the dead man frowned;
But the glare of the sepulchral light,
Perchance had dazzled the warriors sight.

XXII

When the huge stone sunk o'er the tomb,
The night returned in double gloom,
For the moon had gone down, and the stars were
     few;
And, as the Knight and Priest withdrew,
With wavering steps and dizzy brain,
They hardly might the postern gain.
'Tis said, as through the aisles they passed,
They heard strange noises on the blast;
And through the cloister galleries small,
Which at mid-height thread the chancel wall,
Loud sobs, and laughter louder ran,
And voices unlike the voice of man;

As if the fiends kept holiday,
Because these spells were brought to day.
I cannot tell how the truth may be;
I say the tale as 'twas said to me.

XXIII

"Now, hie thee hence," the father said,
"And, when we are on death-bed laid,
O may our dear Ladye, and sweet St John,
Forgive our souls for the deed we have done!"—
　The Monk returned him to his cell,
　　And many a prayer and penance sped;
　When the convent met at the noontide bell—
　　The Monk of St Mary's aisle was dead!
Before the cross was the body laid,
With hands clasped fast, as if still he prayed.

XXIV

The Knight breathed free in the morning wind,
And strove his hardihood to find:
He was glad when he passed the tombstones
　gray,
Which girdle round the fair Abbaye;
For the mystic Book, to his bosom prest,
Felt like a load upon his breast;
And his joints, with nerves of iron twined,
Shook, like the aspen leaves in wind.
Full fain was he when the dawn of day
Began to brighten Cheviot gray;

He joyed to see the chearful light,
And he said Ave Mary, as well as he might.

XXV

The sun had brightened Cheviot gray,
    The sun had brightened the Carter's * side;
And soon beneath the rising day
    Smiled Branksome towers and Teviot's tide
The wild birds told their warbling tale,
    And wakened every flower that blows;
And peeped forth the violet pale,
    And spread her breast the mountain rose.
And lovelier than the rose so red,
    Yet paler than the violet pale,
She early left her sleepless bed,
    The fairest maid of Teviotdale.

XXVI

Why does fair Margaret so early awake,
    And don her kirtle so hastilie;
And the silken knots, which in hurry she would
        make,
    Why tremble her slender fingers to tie;
Why does she stop, and look often around,
    As she glides down the secret stair;
And why does she pat the shaggy blood-hound,
    As he rouses him up from his lair;
And, though she passes the postern alone,
Why is not the watchman's bugle blown?

---

* A mountain on the Border of England, above Jedburgh.

XXVII

The ladye steps in doubt and dread,
Lest her watchful mother hear her tread;
The ladye caresses the rough blood-hound,
Lest his voice should waken the castle round;
The watchman's bugle is not blown,
For he was her foster-father's son;
And she glides through the greenwood at dawn
    of light,
To meet Baron Henry, her own true knight.

XXVIII

The Knight and Ladye fair are met,
And under the hawthorn's boughs are set.
A fairer pair were never seen
To meet beneath the hawthorn green.
He was stately, and young, and tall;
Dreaded in battle, and loved in hall:
And she, when love, scarce told, scarce hid,
Lent to her cheek a livelier red;
When the half sigh her swelling breast
Against the silken ribband pressed;
When her blue eyes their secret told,
Though shaded by her locks of gold—
Where would you find the peerless fair,
With Margaret of Branksome might compare!

XXIX

And now, fair dames, methinks I see
You listen to my minstrelsy;

Your waving locks ye backward throw,
And sidelong bend your necks of snow:—
Ye ween to hear a melting tale,
Of two true lovers in a dale;
   And how the Knight, with tender fire,
     To paint his faithful passion strove;
   Swore he might at her feet expire,
     But never, never cease to love;
And how she blushed, and how she sighed,
And, half consenting, half denied,
And said that she would die a maid;—
Yet, might the bloody feud be stayed,
Henry of Cranstoun, and only he,
Margaret of Branksome's choice should be.

XXX

Alas! fair dames, your hopes are vain!
My harp has lost the enchanting strain;
   Its lightness would my age reprove:
My hairs are gray, my limbs are old,
My heart is dead, my veins are cold:—
   I may not, must not, sing of love.

XXXI

Beneath an oak, mossed o'er by eld,
The Baron's Dwarf his courser held,
   And held his crested helm and spear:
That Dwarf was scarcely an earthly man,
If the tales were true, that of him ran
   Through all the Border, far and near.

'Twas said, when the Baron a-hunting rode
Through Reedsdale's glens, but rarely trod,
    He heard a voice cry, "Lost! lost! lost!'
    And, like tennis-ball by raquet tossed,
        A leap, of thirty feet and three,
Made from the gorse this elfin shape,
Distorted like some dwarfish ape,
        And lighted at Lord Cranstoun's knee.
    Lord Cranstoun was some whit dismayed;
    'Tis said that five good miles he rade,
        To rid him of his company;
But where he rode one mile, the Dwarf ran four,
And the Dwarf was first at the castle door.

XXXII

Use lessens marvel, it is said.
This elvish Dwarf with the Baron staid;
Little he ate, and less he spoke,
Nor mingled with the menial flock;
And oft apart his arms he tossed,
And often muttered, "Lost! lost! lost!"
    He was waspish, arch, and litherlie,
    But well Lord Cranstoun served he:
And he of his service was full fain;
For once he had been ta'en or slain,
    An' it had not been his ministry.
All, between Home and Hermitage,
Talked of Lord Cranstoun's Goblin-Page.

XXXIII

For the Baron went on pilgrimage,
And took with him this elvish Page,
   To Mary's chapel of the Lowes:
For there, beside Our Ladye's lake,
An offering he had sworn to make,
   And he would pay his vows.
But the Ladye of Branksome gathered a band
Of the best that would ride at her command;
   The trysting place was Newark Lee.
Wat of Harden came thither amain,
And thither came John of Thirlestaine,
And thither came William of Deloraine;
   They were three hundred spears and three.
Through Douglas-burn, up Yarrow stream,
Their horses prance, their lances gleam.
They came to St Mary's lake ere day;
But the chapel was void, and the Baron away.
They burned the chapel for very rage,
And cursed Lord Cranstoun's Goblin-Page.

XXXIV

And now, in Branksome's good green-wood,
As under the aged oak he stood,
The Baron's courser pricks his ears,
As if a distant noise he hears.
The Dwarf waves his long lean arm on high,
And signs to the lovers to part and fly;
No time was then to vow or sigh.

Fair Margaret, through the hazel grove,
Flew like the startled cushat-dove: *
The Dwarf the stirrup held and rein;
Vaulted the knight on his steed amain,
And, pondering deep that morning's scene,
Rode eastward through the hawthorns green.

———

WHILE thus he poured the lengthened tale,
The Minstrel's voice began to fail:
Full slyly smiled the observant page,
And gave the withered hand of age
A goblet, crowned with mighty wine,
The blood of Velez' scorched vine.
He raised the silver cup on high,
And, while the big drop filled his eye,
Prayed God to bless the Duchess long,
And all who cheered a son of song.
The attending maidens smiled to see,
How long, how deep, how zealously,
The precious juice the Minstrel quaffed;
And he, emboldened by the draught,
Looked gaily back to them and laughed.
The cordial nectar of the bowl
Swelled his old veins, and cheered his soul;
A lighter, livelier prelude ran,
Ere thus his tale again began.

* Wood pigeon.

THE

LAY OF THE LAST MINSTREL

CANTO THIRD

———

I

AND said I that my limbs were old;
And said I that my blood was cold,
And that my kindly fire was fled,
And my poor withered heart was dead,
  And that I might not sing of love?—
How could I to the dearest theme,
That ever warmed a minstrel's dream,
  So foul, so false, a recreant prove!
How could I name love's very name,
Nor wake my heart to notes of flame!

II

In peace, Love tunes the shepherd's reed;
In war, he mounts the warrior's steed;
In halls, in gay attire is seen;
In hamlets, dances on the green.
Love rules the court, the camp, the grove,
And men below, and saints above;
For love is heaven, and heaven is love.

III

So thought Lord Cranstoun, as I ween,
While, pondering deep the tender scene,
He rode through Branksome's hawthorn green.
　　But the Page shouted wild and shrill—
　　　　And scarce his helmet could he don.
　　When downward from the shady hill
　　　　A stately knight came pricking on.
That warrior's steed, so dapple-gray,
Was dark with sweat, and splashed with clay;
　　His armour red with many a stain:
He seemed in such a weary plight,
As if he had ridden the live-long night;
　　For it was William of Deloraine.

IV

But no whit weary did he seem,
When, dancing in the sunny beam,
He marked the crane on the Baron's crest;
For his ready spear was in his rest.
　　Few were the words, and stern and high,
　　　　That marked the foemen's feudal hate;
　　For question fierce, and proud reply,
　　　　Gave signal soon of dire debate.
Their very coursers seemed to know
That each was other's mortal foe;
And snorted fire, when wheeled around,
To give each knight his vantage ground.

V

In rapid round the Baron bent;
   He sighed a sigh, and prayed a prayer:
The prayer was to his patron saint,
   The sigh was to his ladye fair.
Stout Deloraine nor sighed, nor prayed,
Nor saint, nor ladye, called to aid;
But he stooped his head, and couched his spear,
And spurred his steed to fall career.
The meeting of these champions proud
Seemed like the bursting thunder-cloud.

VI

Stern was the dint the Borderer lent!
The stately Baron backwards bent;
Bent backwards to his horse's tail,
And his plumes went scattering on the gale;
The tough ash spear, so stout and true,
Into a thousand flinders flew.
But Cranstoun's lance, of more avail,
Pierced through, like silk, the Borderer's mail;
Through shield, and jack, and acton past.
Deep in his bosom broke at last.—
Still sate the warrior saddle-fast,
Till, stumbling in the mortal shock,
Down went the steed, the girthing broke,
Hurled on a heap lay man and horse.
The Baron onward passed his course;
Nor knew—so giddy rolled his brain—
His foe lay stretched upon the plain.

VII

But when he reined his courser round,
And saw his foeman on the ground
   Lie senseless as the bloody clay,
He bade his Page to staunch the wound,
   And there beside the warrior stay.
And tend him in his doubtful state,
And lead him to Branksome castle-gate:
His noble mind was inly moved
For the kinsman of the maid he loved.
"This shaft thou do without delay;
No longer here myself may stay:
Unless the swifter I speed away,
Short shrift will be at my dying day."—

VIII

Away in speed Lord Cranstoun rode;
The Goblin-Page behind abode:
His lord's command he ne'er withstood,
Though small his pleasure to do good.
As the corslet off he took,
The Dwarf espied the Mighty Book!
Much he marvelled, a knight of pride
Like a book-bosomed priest should ride:
He thought not to search or staunch the wound,
Until the secret he had found.

IX

The iron band, the iron clasp,
Resisted long the elfin grasp;
For when the first he had undone,
It closed as he the next begun.
Those iron clasps, that iron band,
Would not yield to unchristened hand,
Till he smeared the cover o'er
With the Borderer's curdled gore;
A moment then the volume spread,
And one short spell therein he read.
It had much of glamour * might,
Could make a ladye seem a knight;
The cobwebs on a dungeon wall
Seem tapestry in lordly hall;
A nut-shell seem a gilded barge,
A sheeling † seem a palace large,
And youth seem age, and age seem youth—
All was delusion, nought was truth.

X

He had not read another spell,
When on his cheek a buffet fell,
So fierce, it stretched him on the plain,
Beside the wounded Deloraine.
From the ground he rose dismayed,
And shook his huge and matted head;

* Magical delusion.
† A shepherd's but.

One word he muttered, and no more—
"Man of age, thou smitest sore!"—
No more the Elfin Page durst try
Into the wonderous Book to pry;
The clasps, though smeared with Christian gore,
Shut faster than they were before.
He hid it underneath his cloak.—
Now, if you ask who gave the stroke,
I cannot tell, so mot I thrive;
It was not given by man alive.

XI

Unwillingly himself he addressed,
To do his master's high behest:
He lifted up the living corse,
And laid it on the weary horse;
He led him into Branksome hall,
Before the beards of the warders all;
And each did after swear and say,
There only passed a wain of hay.
He took him to Lord David's tower,
Even to the Ladye's secret bower;
And, but that stronger spells were spread,
And the door might not be opened,
He had laid him on her very bed.
Whate'er he did of gramarye, *
Was always done maliciously;
He flung the warrior on the ground,
And the blood welled freshly from the wound.

---

*   Magic.

XII

As he repassed the outer court,
He spied the fair young child at sport:
He thought to train him to the wood;
For, at a word, be it understood,
He was always for ill, and never for good.
Seemed to the boy, some comrade gay
Led him forth to the woods to play;
On the draw-bridge the warders stout
Saw a terrier and lurcher passing out.

XIII

He led the boy o'er bank and fell,
    Until they came to a woodland brook;
The running stream dissolved the spell,
    And his own elvish shape he took.
Could he have had his pleasure vilde,
He had crippled the joints of the noble child;
Or, with his fingers long and lean,
Had strangled him in fiendish spleen:
But his awful mother he had in dread,
And also his power was limited;
So he but scowled on the startled child,
And darted through the forest wild;
The woodland brook he bounding crossed,
And laughed, and shouted, "Lost! lost! lost!"—

XIV

Full sore amazed at the wondrous change,
　　And frightened, as a child might be;
At the wild yell and visage strange,
　　And the dark words of gramarye,
The child, amidst the forest bower,
Stood rooted like a lilye flower;
　　And when at length, with trembling pace,
　　　　He sought to find where Branksome lay,
　　He feared to see that grisly face
　　　　Glare from some thicket on his way.
Thus, starting oft, he journeyed on,
And deeper in the wood is gone,—
For aye the more he sought his way,
The farther still he went astray,—
Until he heard the mountains round
Ring to the baying of a hound.

XV

And hark! and hark! the deep-mouthed bark
　　Comes nigher still, and nigher;
Bursts on the path a dark blood-hound,
His tawny muzzle tracked the ground,
　　And his red eye shot fire.
Soon as the wildered child saw he,
He flew at him right furiouslie.
I ween you would have seen with joy
The bearing of the gallant boy,

When, worthy of his noble sire,
His wet cheek glowed 'twixt fear and ire!
He faced the blood-hound manfully,
And held his little bat on high;
So fierce he struck, the dog, afraid,
At cautious distance hoarsely bayed,
    But still in act to spring;
When dashed an archer through the glade,
And when he saw the hound was stayed,
    He drew his tough bow-string;
But a rough voice cried, "Shoot not, hoy!
Ho! shoot not, Edward—'tis a boy."—

XVI

The speaker issued from the wood,
And checked his fellow's surly mood,
    And quelled the ban-dog's ire;
He was an English yeoman good,
    And born in Lancashire.
Well could he hit a fallow deer
    Five hundred feet him fro;
With hand more true, and eye more clear,
    No archer bended bow.
His coal-black hair, shorn round and close,
    Set off his sun-burned face;
Old England's sign, St George's cross,
    His barret-cap did grace;
His hugle-horn hung by his side,
    All in a wolf-skin baldric tied;

And his short faulchion, sharp and clear,
Had pierced the throat of many a deer.

XVII

His kirtle, made of forest green,
    Reached scantly to his knee;
And, at his belt, of arrows keen
    A furbished sheaf bore he;
His buckler scarce in breadth a span,
    No longer fence had he;
He never counted him a man,
    Would strike below the knee;
His slackened bow was in his hand,
And the leash, that was his blood-hound's band.

XVIII

He would not do the fair child harm,
But held him with his powerful arm,
That he might neither fight nor flee;
For when the Red-Cross spied he,
The boy strove long and violently.
"Now, by St George," the archer cries,
"Edward, methinks we have a prize!
This boy's fair face, and courage free,
Shews he is come of high degree."—

XIX

    "Yes! I am come of high degree,
    For I am the heir of bold Buccleuch;
And, if thou dost not set me free,
    False Southron, thou shalt dearly rue!

For Walter of Harden shall come with speed,
And William of Deloraine, good at need,
And every Scott from Esk to Tweed;
And, if thou dost not let me go,
Despite thy arrows, and thy bow,
I'll have thee hanged to feed the crow!"—

XX

"Gramercy, for thy good will, fair boy!
My mind was never set so high;
But if thou art chief of such a clan,
And art the son of such a man,
And ever comest to thy command,
   Our wardens had need to keep good order:
My bow of yew to a hazel wand,
   Thou'lt make them work upon the Border.
Meantime, be pleased to come with me,
For good Lord Dacre shalt thou see;
I think our work is well begun,
When we have taken thy father's son."—

XXI

Although the child was led away,
In Branksome still he seemed to stay,
For so the Dwarf his part did play;
And, in the shape of that young boy,
He wrought the castle much annoy.
The comrades of the young Buccleuch
He pinched, and beat, and overthrew;
Nay, some of them he well nigh slew.

He tore Dame Maudlin's silken tire,
And, as Sym Hall stood by the fire,
He lighted the match of his bandelier, *
And woefully scorched the hackbutteer. †
It may be hardly thought or said,
The mischief that the urchin made,
Till many of the castle guessed,
That the young Baron was possessed!

XXII

Well I ween, the charm he held
The noble Ladye had soon dispelled;
But she was deeply busied then
To tend the wounded Deloraine.
    Much she wondered to find him lie,
        On the stone threshold stretched along;
    She thought some spirit of the sky
        Had done the bold moss-trooper wrong,
Because, despite her precept dread,
Perchance he in the Book had read;
But the broken lance in his bosom stood,
And it was earthly steel and wood.

XXIII

She drew the splinter from the wound,
    And with a charm she staunched the blood;
She bade the gash be cleansed and bound:
    No longer by his couch she stood;

---

*   *Bandelier*, belt for carrying ammunition.
†   *Hackbutteer*, musketeer.

But she has ta'en the broken lance,
 And washed it from the clotted gore,
 And salved the splinter o'er and o'er.
William of Deloraine, in trance,
 Whene'er she turned it round and round,
 Twisted, as if she galled his wound.
 Then to her maidens she did say,
 That he should be whole man and sound,
 Within the course of a night and day.
Full long she toiled; for she did rue
Mishap to friend so stout and true.

XXIV

So passed the day—the evening fell,
'Twas near the time of curfew-bell;
The air was mild, the wind was calm,
The stream was smooth, the dew was balm;
E'en the rude watchman, on the tower,
Enjoyed and blessed the lovely hour.
Far more fair Margaret loved and blessed
The hour of silence and of rest.
On the high turret sitting lone,
She waked at times the lute's soft tone;
Touched a wild note, and all between
Thought of the bower of hawthorns green.
Her golden hair streamed free from band,
Her fair cheek rested on her hand,
Her blue eyes sought the west afar,
For lovers love the western star.

XXV

Is yon the star, o'er Penchryst Pen,
That rises slowly to her ken,
And, spreading broad its wavering light,
Shakes its loose tresses on the night ?
Is yon red glare the western star?—
O, 'tis the beacon-blaze of war!
Scarce could she draw her tightened breath,
For well she knew the fire of death!

XXVI

The Warder viewed it blazing strong,
And blew his war-note loud and long,
Till, at the high and haughty sound,
Rock, wood, and river, rung around.
The blast alarmed the festal hall,
And startled forth the warriors all;
Far downward, in the castle-yard,
Full many a torch and cresset glared;
And helms and plumes, confusedly tossed,
Were in the blaze half-seen, half-lost;
And spears in wild disorder shook,
Like reeds beside a frozen brook.

XXVII

The Seneschal, whose silver hair
Was reddened by the torches' glare,
Stood in the midst, with gesture proud,
And issued forth his mandates loud.—

"On Penchryst glows a bale * of fire,
And three are kindling on Priesthaughswire;
    Ride out, ride out,
    The foe to scout!
Mount, mount for Branksome, † every man!
Thou, Todrig, warn the Johnstone clan,
    That ever are true and stout.—
Ye need not send to Liddesdale;
For, when they see the blazing bale,
Elliots and Armstrongs never fail.—
Ride, Alton, ride, for death and life!
And warn the warden of the strife.
Young Gilbert, let our beacon blaze,
Our kin, and clan, and friends, to raise."—

XXVIII

Fair Margaret, from the turret head,
Heard, far below, the coursers' tread,
    While loud the harness rung,
As to their seats, with clamour dread,
    The ready horsemen sprung;
And trampling hoofs, and iron coats,
And leaders' voices, mingled notes,
    And out! and out!
    In hasty route,

---

*   *bale*, beacon-faggot.
†   *Mount for Banksome* was the gathering word of the Scotts.

The horsemen galloped forth;
Dispersing to the south to scout,
   And east, and west, and north,
To view their coming enemies,
And warn their vassals, and allies.

XXIX

The ready page, with hurried hand,
Awaked the need-fire's * slumbering brand,
   And ruddy blushed the heaven;
For a sheet of flame, from the turret high,
Waved like a blood-flag on the sky,
   All flaring and uneven.
And soon a score of fires, I ween,
From height, and hill, and cliff, were seen;
Each with warlike tidings fraught;
Each from each the signal caught;
Each after each they glanced to sight,
As stars arise upon the night.
They gleamed on many a dusky tarn, †
Haunted by the lonely earn; ‡
On many a cairn's § gray pyramid,
Where urns of mighty chiefs lie hid;
Till high Dunedin the blazes saw,
From Soltra and Dumpender Law;

---

*   *Need-fire*, beacon.
†   *Tarn*, a mountain lake.
‡   *Earn*, the Scottish eagle.
§   *Cairn*, a pile of stones.

And Lothian heard the Regent's order,
That all should bowne * them for the Border.

XXX

The livelong night in Branksome rang
   The ceaseless sound of steel;
The castle-bell, with backward clang,
   Sent forth the larum peal;
Was frequent heard the heavy jar,
Where massy stone and iron bar
Were piled on echoing keep and tower,
To whelm the foe with deadly shower;
Was frequent heard the changing guard,
And watch-word from the sleepless ward;
While, wearied by the endless din,
Blood-hound and ban-dog yelled within.

XXXI

The noble Dame, amid the broil,
Shared the gray Seneschal's high toil,
And spoke of danger with a smile;
Cheered the young knights, and council sage
Held with the chiefs of riper age.

*   *Bowne*, make ready.

No tidings of the foe were brought,
Nor of his numbers knew they ought,
Nor in what time the truce he sought.
   Some said, that there were thousands ten;
And others weened that it was nought
   But Leven Clans, or Tynedale men,
Who came to gather in black mail; *
And Liddisdale, with small avail,
   Might drive them lightly back agen.
So passed the anxious night away,
And welcome was the peep of day.

————

CEASED the high sound—the listening throng
Applaud the Master of the Song;
And marvel much, in helpless age,
So hard should be his pilgrimage.
Had he no friend—no daughter dear,
His wandering toil to share and cheer,
No son, to be his father's stay,
And guide him on the rugged way?—
"Aye! once he had—but he was dead!"
Upon the harp he stooped his head,
And busied himself the strings withal,
To hide the tear, that fain would fall.
In solemn measure, soft and slow,
Arose a father's notes of woe.

---

*   Protection-money exacted by free-booters.

THE

LAY OF THE LAST MINSTREL

CANTO FOURTH

———

I

S w e e t Teviot! on thy silver tide
The glaring bale-fires blaze no more;
No longer steel-clad warriors ride
Along thy wild and willowed shore;
Where'er thou wind'st by dale or hill,
All, all is peaceful, all is still,
　　As if thy waves, since Time was born,
Since first they rolled upon the Tweed,
Had only heard the shepherd's reed,
　　Nor started at the bugle-horn.

II

Unlike the tide of human time,
Which, though it change in ceaseless flow,
Retains each grief, retains each crime,
　　Its earliest course was doomed to know,
And, darker as it downward bears,
Is stained with past and present tears.

Low as that tide has ebbed with me,
It still reflects to memory's eye
The hour, my brave, my only boy,
    Fell by the side of great Dundee.
Why, when the volleying musket played
Against the bloody Highland blade,
Why was not I beside him laid!—
Enough—he died the death of fame;
Enough—he died with conquering Graeme.

III

Now over Border dale and fell,
    Full wide and far was terror spread;
For pathless marsh, and mountain cell,
    The peasant left his lowly shed.
The frightened flocks and herds were pent
Beneath the peel's rude battlement;
And maids and matrons dropped the tear,
While ready warriors seized the spear.
From Branksome's towers, the watchman's eye
Dun wreaths of distant smoke can spy,
Which, curling in the rising sun,
Shewed southern ravage was begun.

IV

Now loud the heedful gate-ward cried—
    "Prepare ye all for blows and blood!
Watt Tinlinn, from the Liddel-side,
    Comes wading through the flood.

Full oft the Tynedale snatchers knock
At his lone gate, and prove the lock;
It was but last St Barnabright
They sieged him a whole summer night,
But fled at morning; well they knew,
In vain he never twanged the yew.
Right sharp has been the evening shower,
That drove him from his Liddel tower;
And, by my faith," the gate-ward said,
"I think, 'twill prove a Warden-Raid." *

V

While thus he spoke, the bold yeoman
Entered the echoing barbican.
He led a small and shaggy nag,
That through a bog, from hag to hag, †
Could bound like any Bilhope stag.
It bore his wife and children twain;
A half-clothed serf ‡ was all their train:
His wife, stout, ruddy, and dark-browed,
Of silver broach and bracelet proud,
Laughed to her friends among the crowd.
He was of stature passing tall,
But sparely formed, and lean withal:
A battered morion on his brow;
A leathern jack, as fence enow,

---

* An inroad commanded by the Warden in person.
† The broken ground in a bog.
‡ Bonds-man.

On his broad shoulders loosely hung;
A border-axe behind was slung;
    His spear, six Scottish ells in length,
Seemed newly dyed with gore;
    His shafts and bow, of wondrous strength,
His hardy partner bore.

VI

Thus to the Ladye did Tinlinn shew
The tidings of the English foe:—
"Belted Will Howard is marching here,
And hot Lord Dacre, with many a spear,
And all the German hagbut-men, *
Who have long lain at Askerten:
They crossed the Liddel at curfew hour,
And burned my little lonely tower;
The fiend receive their souls therefor!
It had not been burned this year and more.
Barn-yard and dwelling, blazing bright,
Served to guide me on my flight;
But I was chased the live-long night.
Black John of Akeshaw, and Fergus Graeme,
Fast upon my traces came,
Until I turned at Priesthaugh Scrogg,
And shot their horses in the bog,
Slew Fergus with my lance outright—
I had him long at high despite:
He drove my cows last Fastern's night."—

* Musketeers

VII

Now weary scouts from Liddesdale,
Fast hurrying in, confirmed the tale;
   As far as they could judge by ken,
     Three hours would bring to Teviot's strand
   Three thousand armed Englishmen.—
     Meanwhile, full many a warlike band,
From Teviot, Aill, and Ettrick shade,
Came in, their Chief's defence to aid.
There was saddling and mounting in haste,
   There was pricking o'er moor and lee;
He, that was last at the trysting place,
   Was but lightly held of his gay ladye.

VIII

From fair St Mary's silver wave,
   From dreary Gamescleuch's dusky height,
His ready lances Thirlestane brave
   Arrayed beneath a banner bright.
The tressured fleur-de-luce he claims
To wreathe his shield, since royal James,
Encamped by Fala's mossy wave,
The proud distinction grateful gave,
   For faith mid feudal jars;
What time, save Thirlestane alone,
Of Scotland's stubborn barons none
   Would march to southern wars;
And hence, in fair remembrance worn,
Yon sheaf of spears his crest has borne;

Hence his high motto shines revealed,—
"Ready, aye ready," for the field.

IX

An aged knight, to danger steeled,
    With many a moss-trooper, came on;
And azure in a golden field,
The stars and crescent graced his shield,
        Without the bend of Murdieston.
Wide lay his lands round Oakwood tower,
And wide round haunted Castle-Ower;
High over Borthwick's mountain flood,
His wood-embosomed mansion stood;
In the dark glen, so deep below,
The herds of plundered England low,
His bold retainers' daily food,
And bought with danger, blows, and blood.
Marauding chief! his sole delight
The moonlight raid, the morning fight;
Not even the Flower of Yarrow's charms,
In youth, might tame his rage for arms;
And still, in age, he spurned at rest,
And still his brows the helmet pressed,
Albeit the blanched locks below
Were white as Dinlay's spotless snow:
    Five stately warriors drew the sword
        Before their father's band;
    A braver knight than Harden's lord
        Ne'er belted on a brand.

X

Scotts of Eskdale, a stalwart band,
   Came trooping down the Todshawhill;
By the sword they won their land,
   And by the sword they hold it still.
Hearken, Ladye, to the tale,
How thy sires won fair Eskdale.—
Earl Morton was lord of that valley fair,
The Beattisons were his vassals there.
The Earl was gentle, and mild of mood,
The vassals were warlike, and fierce, and rude;
High of heart, and haughty of word,
Little they recked of a tame liege-lord.
The Earl to fair Eskdale came,
Homage and seignory to claim:
Of Gilbert the Galliard, a heriot * he sought,
Saying, "Give thy best steed, as a vassal ought."
—"Dear to me is my bonny white steed,
Oft has he helped me at pinch of need;
Lord and Earl though thou be, I trow,
I can rein Bucksfoot better than thou."—
Word on word gave fuel to fire,
Till so highly blazed the Beattison's ire,
But that the Earl the flight had ta'en,
The vassals there their lord had slain.
Sore he plied both whip and spur,
As he urged his steed through Eskdale muir;

* The feudal superior, in certain cases, was entitled to the best horse of the vassal, in name of Heriot, or Herezeld.

And it fell down a weary weight,
Just on the threshold of Branksome gate.

XI

The Earl was a wrathful man to see!
Full fain avenged would he be.
In haste to Branksome's lord he spoke,
Saying—"Take these traitors to thy yoke;
For a cast of hawks, and a purse of gold,
All Eskdale I'll sell thee, to have and hold:
Beshrew thy heart, of the Beattisons' clan
If thou leavest on Eske a landed man!
But spare Woodkerrick's lands alone,
For he lent me his horse to escape upon."—
A glad man then was Branksome bold!
Down he flung him the purse of gold.
To Eskdale soon he spurred amain,
And with him five hundred riders has ta'en.
He left his merrymen in the mist of the hill,
And bade them hold them close and still;
And alone he wended to the plain,
To meet with the Galliard and all his train.
To Gilbert the Galliard thus he said:—
"Know thou me for thy liege-lord and head;
Deal not with me as with Morton tame,
For Scotts play best at the roughest game.
Give me in peace my heriot due,
Thy bonny white steed, or thou shalt rue.
If my horn I three times wind,
Eskdale shall long have the sound in mind."—

XII

Loudly the Beattison laughed in scorn;—
"Little care we for thy winded horn.
Ne'er shall it be the Galliard's lot,
To yield his steed to a haughty Scott.
Wend thou to Branksome back on foot,
With rusty spur and miry boot."—
He blew his bugle so loud and hoarse,
That the dun deer started at far Craikcross;
He blew again so loud and clear,
Through the gray mountain-mist there did lances
        appear;
And the third blast rang with such a din,
That the echoes answered from Pentoun-linn,
And all his riders came lightly in.
Then had you seen a gallant shock,
When saddles were emptied, and lances broke!
For each scornful word the Galliard had said,
A Beattison on the field was laid.
His own good sword the chieftain drew,
And he bore the Galliard through and through;
Where the Beattisons' blood mixed with the rill,
The Galliard's Haugh men call it still.
The Scotts have scattered the Beattison clan,
In Eskdale they left but one landed man.
The valley of Eske, from the mouth to the source,
Was lost and won for that bonny white horse.   V

XIII

Whitslade the Hawk, and Headshaw came,
And warriors more than I may name;
From Yarrow-cleuch to Hindhaugh-swair,
　　From Woodhouselie to Chester-glen,
Trooped man and horse, and bow and spear;
　　Their gathering word was Bellenden.
And better hearts o'er Border sod
To siege or rescue never rode.
　　The Ladye marked the aids come in,
　　　　And high her heart of pride arose:
　　She bade her youthful son attend,
　　That he might know his father's friend,
　　　　And learn to face his foes.
　　　　"The boy is ripe to look on war;
　　　　I saw him draw a cross-bow stiff,
　　And his true arrow struck afar
　　　　The raven's nest upon the cliff.
The Red Cross, on a southern breast,
Is broader than the raven's nest:
Thou, Whitslade, shalt teach him his weapon to
　　wield,
And o'er him hold his fathers shield."—

XIV

Well may you think, the wily Page
Cared not to face the Ladye sage.
He counterfeited childish fear,
And shrieked, and shed full many a tear,

And moaned and plained in manner wild.
   The attendants to the Ladye told,
  Some fairy, sure, had changed the child,
   That wont to be so free and bold.
Then wrathful was the noble dame;
She blushed blood-red for very shame:—
"Hence! ere the clan his faintness view;
Hence with the weakling to Buccleuch!—
Watt Tinlinn, thou shalt be his guide
To Rangleburn's lonely side.—
Sure some fell fiend has cursed our line,
That coward should e'er be son of mine!"—

XV

A heavy task Watt Tinlinn had,
To guide the counterfeited lad.
Soon as his palfrey felt the weight
Of that ill-omen'd elvish freight,
He bolted, sprung, and reared amain,
Nor heeded bit, nor curb, nor rein.
  It cost Watt Tinlinn mickle toil
  To drive him but a Scottish mile;
   But, as a shallow brook they crossed,
  The elf, amid the running stream,
  His figure changed, like form in dream,
   And fled, and shouted, "Lost! lost! lost!"
Full fast the urchin ran and laughed,
But faster still a cloth-yard shaft

Whistled from startled Tinlinn's yew,
And pierced his shoulder through and through.
Although the imp might not be slain,
And though the wound soon healed again,
Yet, as he ran, he yelled for pain;
And Watt of Tinlinn, much aghast,
Rode back to Branksome fiery fast.

XVI

Soon on the hill's steep verge he stood,
That looks o'er Branksome's towers and wood;
And martial murmurs, from below,
Proclaimed the approaching southern foe.
Through the dark wood, in mingled tone,
Were Border-pipes and bugles blown;
The coursers' neighing he could ken,
And measured tread of marching men;
While broke at times the solemn hum,
The Almayn's sullen kettle-drum;
    And banners tall, of crimson sheen,
        Above the copse appear;
    And, glistening through the hawthorns green,
        Shine helm, and shield, and spear.

XVII

Light forayers first, to view the ground,
Spurred their fleet coursers loosely round;
    Behind, in close array, and fast,
        The Kendal archers, all in green,
    Obedient to the bugle-blast,
        Advancing from the wood are seen.

To back and guard the archer band,
Lord Dacre's bill-men were at hand:
A hardy race, on Irthing bred,
With kirtles white, and crosses red,
Arrayed beneath the banner tall,
That streamed o'er Acre's conquered wall;
And minstrels, as they marched in order,
Played, "Noble Lord Dacre, he dwells on the
    Border."

XVIII

Behind the English bill and bow,
The mercenaries, firm and slow,
    Moved on to fight, in dark array,
By Conrad led of Wolfenstein,
Who brought the band from distant Rhine,
    And sold their blood for foreign pay.
The camp their home, their law the sword,
They knew no country, owned no lord:
They were not armed like England's sons,
But bore the levin-darting guns;
Buff-coats, all frounced and 'broidered o'er,
And morsing horns * and scarfs they wore;
Each better knee was bared, to aid
The warriors in the escalade;
All, as they marched, in rugged tongue,
Songs of Teutonic feuds they sung.

---

*   Powder-flasks

XIX

But louder still the clamour grew,
And louder still the minstrels blew,
When, from beneath the greenwood tree,
Rode forth Lord Howard's chivalry;
His men at arms, with glaive and spear,
Brought up the battle's glittering rear.
There many a youthful knight, full keen
To gain his spurs, in arms was seen,
With favour in his crest, or glove,
Memorial of his ladye-love.
So rode they forth in fair array,
Till full their lengthened lines display;
Then called a halt, and made a stand,
And cried, "St George, for merry England!"—

XX

Now every English eye, intent,
On Branksome's armed towers was bent.
So near they were, that they might know
The straining harsh of each cross-bow;
On battlement and bartizan
Gleamed axe, and spear, and partizan;
Falcon and culver, * on each tower,
Stood prompt their deadly hail to shower;
And flashing armour frequent broke
From eddying whirls of sable smoke,

* Ancient pieces of artillery.

Where, upon tower and turret head,
The seething pitch and molten lead
Reeked, like a witch's cauldron red.
While yet they gaze, the bridges fall,
The wicket opes, and from the wall
Rides forth the hoary Seneschal.

XXI

Armed he rode, all save the head,
His white beard o'er his breast-plate spread;
Unbroke by age, erect his seat,
He ruled his eager courser's gait;
Forced him, with chastened fire, to prance,
And, high curvetting, slow advance:
In sign of truce, his better hand
Displayed a peeled willow-wand;
His squire, attending in the rear,
Bore high a gauntlet on a spear.
When they espied him riding out,
Lord Howard and Lord Dacre stout
Sped to the front of their array,
To hear what this old knight should say.

XXII

"Ye English warden lords, of you
Demands the Ladye of Buccleuch,
Why, 'gainst the truce of Border-tide,
In hostile guise ye dare to ride,

With Kendal bow, and Gilsland brand,
And all yon mercenary band,
Upon the bounds of fair Scotland ?
My Ladye reads you swith return;
And, if but one poor straw you burn,
Or do our towers so much molest,
As scare one swallow from her nest,—
St Mary! but we'll light a brand,
Shall warm your hearths in Cumberland."—

XXIII

A wrathful man was Dacre's lord,
But calmer Howard took the word:—
"May't please thy Dame, Sir Seneschal,
To seek the castle's outward wall,
Our pursuivant-at-arms shall shew,
Both why we came, and when we go."—
The message sped, the noble Dame
To the walls' outward circle came;
Each chief around leaned on his spear,
To see the pursuivant appear.
All in Lord Howard's livery dressed,
The lion argent decked his breast;
He led a boy of blooming hue—
O sight to meet a mother's view!
It was the heir of great Buccleuch.
Obeisance meet the herald made,
And thus his master's will he said:—

XXIV

"It irks, high Dame, my noble Lords,
'Gainst ladye fair to draw their swords;
But yet they may not tamely see,
All through the western wardenry,
Your law-contemning kinsmen ride,
And burn and spoil the Border-side;
And ill beseems your rank and birth
To make your towers a flemens-firth. *
We claim from thee William of Deloraine,
That he may suffer march-treason pain: †
It was but last St Cuthbert's even,
He pricked to Stapleton on Leven,
Harried ‡ the lands of Richard Musgrave,
And slew his brother by dint of glaive.
Then, since a lone and widowed Dame
These restless riders may not tame,
Either receive within thy towers
Two hundred of my master's powers,
Or straight they sound their warison, §
And storm and spoil thy garrison;
And this fair boy, to London led,
Shall good King Edward's page be bred."—

* An asylum for outlaws.
† Border treason.
‡ Plundered.
§ Note of assault.

XXV

He ceased—and loud the boy did cry,
And stretched his little arms on high;
Implored for aid each well-known face,
And strove to seek the Dame's embrace.
A moment changed that Ladye's cheer,
Gushed to her eye the unbidden tear;
She gazed upon the leaders round,
And dark and sad each warrior frowned;
Then, deep within her sobbing breast
She locked the struggling sigh to rest;
Unaltered and collected stood,
And thus replied, in dauntless mood:—

XXVI

"Say to your Lords of high emprize,
Who war on women and on boys,
That either William of Deloraine
Will cleanse him, by oath, of march-treason stain,
Or else he will the combat take
'Gainst Musgrave, for his honour's sake.
No knight in Cumberland so good,
But William may count with him kin and blood.
Knighthood he took of Douglas' sword,
When English blood swelled Ancram ford;
And but that Lord Dacre's steed was wight,
And bare him ably in the flight,
Himself had seen him dubbed a knight.

For the young heir of Branksome's line,
God be his aid, and God be mine!
Through me no friend shall meet his doom;
Here, while I live, no foe finds room.
   Then, if thy lords their purpose urge,
      Take our defiance loud and high;
Our slogan is their lyke-wake * dirge,
      Our moat, the grave where they shall lie."—

XXVII

Proud she looked round, applause to claim—
Then lightened Thirlestane's eye of flame;
   His bugle Watt of Harden blew;
Pensils and pennons wide were flung,
To heaven the Border slogan rung,
   "St Mary for the young Buccleuch!"—
The English war-cry answered wide,
   And forward bent each southern spear;
Each Kendal archer made a stride,
   And drew the bow-string to his ear;
Each minstrel's war-note loud was blown;—
But, e'er a gray-goose shaft had flown,
   A horseman galloped from the rear.

XXVIII

"Ah! noble Lords!" he, breathless, said,
"What treason has your march betrayed?

---

*   *Lyke-wake*, the watching a corpse previous to interment.

What make you here, from aid so far,
Before you walls, around you war?
Your foemen triumph in the thought,
That in the toils the lion's caught.
Already on dark Ruberslaw
The Douglas holds his weapon-schaw; *
The lances, waving in his train,
Clothe the dun heath like autumn grain;
And on the Liddel's northern strand,
To bar retreat to Cumberland,
Lord Maxwell ranks his merry-men good,
Beneath the eagle and the rood;
　　And Jedwood, Eske, and Teviotdale,
　　　　Have to proud Angus come;
　　And all the Merse and Lauderdale
　　　　Have risen with haughty Home.
　　An exile from Northumberland,
　　　　In Liddesdale I've wandered long;
　　But still my heart was with merry England,
　　　　And cannot brook my country's wrong;
And hard I've spurred all night, to shew
The mustering of the coming foe."—

XXIX

"And let them come!" fierce Dacre cried;
"For soon yon crest, my father's pride,
That swept the shores of Judah's sea,
And waved in gales of Galilee,

* *Weapon-schaw*, the military array of a country.

From Branksome's highest towers displayed,
Shall mock the rescue's lingering aid!—
Level each harquebuss on row;
Draw, merry archers, draw the bow;
Up, bill-men, to the walls, and cry,
Dacre for England, win or die!"—

XXX

"Yet hear," quoth Howard, "calmly hear,
Nor deem my words the words of fear:
For who, in field or foray slack,
Saw the blanche lion e'er fall back?
But thus to risque our Border flower
In strife against a kingdom's power,
Ten thousand Scots 'gainst thousands three,
Certes, were desperate policy.
Nay, take the terms the Ladye made,
E'er conscious of the advancing aid:
Let Musgrave meet fierce Deloraine
In single fight; and if he gain,
He gains for us; but if he's crossed,
'Tis but a single warrior lost:
The rest, retreating as they came,
Avoid defeat, and death, and shame."—

XXXI

Ill could the haughty Dacre brook
His brother-warden's sage rebuke;
And yet his forward step he staid,
And slow and sullenly obeyed.

But ne'er again the Border side
Did these two lords in friendship ride;
And this slight discontent, men say,
Cost blood upon another day.   ✓

XXXII

The pursuivant-at-arms again
    Before the castle took his stand;
His trumpet called, with parleying strain,
    The leaders of the Scottish band;
And he defied, in Musgrave's right,
Stout Deloraine to single fight;
A gauntlet at their feet he laid,
And thus the terms of fight he said:—
"If in the lists good Musgrave's sword
    Vanquish the Knight of Deloraine,
Your youthful chieftain, Branksome's lord,
    Shall hostage for his clan remain:
If Deloraine foil good Musgrave,
The boy his liberty shall have.
    Howe'er it falls, the English band,
Unharming Scots, by Scots unharmed,
In peaceful march, like men unarmed,
    Shall straight retreat to Cumberland."—

XXXIII

Unconscious of the near relief,
The proffer pleased each Scottish chief,
    Though much the Ladye sage gainsayed;

For though their hearts were brave and true,
From Jedwood's recent sack they knew,
   How tardy was the Regent's aid:
And you may guess the noble Dame
   Durst not the secret prescience own,
Sprung from the art she might not name,
   By which the coming help was known.
Closed was the compact, and agreed,
That lists should be inclosed with speed,
   Beneath the castle on a lawn:
They fixed the morrow for the strife,
On foot, with Scottish axe and knife,
   At the fourth hour from peep of dawn;
When Deloraine, from sickness freed,
Or else a champion in his stead,
Should for himself and chieftain stand,
Against stout Musgrave, hand to hand.

XXXIV

I know right well, that, in their lay,
Full many minstrels sing and say,
   Such combat should be made on horse,
On foaming steed, in full career,
With brand to aid, when as the spear
   Should shiver in the course:
But he, the jovial Harper, taught
Me, yet a youth, how it was fought,

In guise which now I say;
He knew each ordinance and clause
Of black Lord Archibald's battle-laws,
   In the old Douglas' day.
He brooked not, he, that scoffing tongue
Should tax his minstrelsy with wrong,
   Or call his song untrue:
For this, when they the goblet plied,
And such rude taunt had chafed his pride,
   The bard of Reull he slew.
On Teviot's side, in fight they stood,
And tuneful hands were stained with blood;
Where still the thorn's white branches wave,
Memorial o'er his rival's grave.

XXXV

Why should I tell the rigid doom,
That dragged my master to his tomb;
   How Ousenam's maidens tore their hair,
Wept till their eyes were dead and dim,
And wrung their hands for love of him,
   Who died at Jedwood Air?
He died!—his scholars, one by one,
To the cold silent grave are gone;
And I, alas! survive alone,
To muse o'er rivalries of yore,
And grieve that I shall hear no more
The strains, with envy heard before;

For, with my minstrel brethren fled,
My jealousy of song is dead.

———

HE paused: the listening dames again
Applaud the hoary Minstrel's strain.
With many a word of kindly cheer,—
In pity half, and half sincere,—
Marvelled the Duchess how so well
His legendary song could tell—
Of ancient deeds, so long forgot;
Of feuds, whose memory was not;
Of forests, now laid waste and bare;
Of towers, which harbour now the hare;
Of manners, long since changed and gone;
Of chiefs, who under their gray stone
So long had slept, that fickle Fame
Had blotted from her rolls their name,
And twined round some new minion's head
The fading wreath for which they bled;
In sooth, 'twas strange, this old man's verse
Could call them from their marble hearse.

   The Harper smiled, well-pleased; for ne'er
Was flattery lost on poet's ear:
A simple race! they waste their toil
For the vain tribute of a smile;

E'en when in age their flame expires,
Her dulcet breath can fan its fires:
Their drooping fancy wakes at praise,
And strives to trim the short-lived blaze.

Smiled then, well-pleased, the Aged Man,
And thus his tale continued ran.

THE

LAY OF THE LAST MINSTREL

CANTO FIFTH

I

CALL it not vain:—they do not err,
  Who say, that, when the Poet dies,
Mute Nature mourns her worshipper,
  And celebrates his obsequies;
Who say, tall cliff, and cavern lone,
For the departed bard make moan;
That mountains weep in crystal rill;
That flowers in tears of balm distil;
Through his loved groves that breezes sigh,
And oaks, in deeper groan, reply;
And rivers teach their rushing wave
To murmur dirges round his grave.

II

Not that, in sooth, o'er mortal urn
Those things inanimate can mourn;
But that the stream, the wood, the gale,
Is vocal with the plaintive wail

Of those, who, else forgotten long,
Lived in the poet's faithful song,
And, with the poet's parting breath,
Whose memory feels a second death.
The Maid's pale shade, who wails her lot,
That love, true love, should be forgot,
From rose and hawthorn shakes the tear
Upon the gentle minstrel's bier:
The Phantom Knight, his glory fled,
Mourns o'er the field he heap'd * with dead;
Mounts the wild blast that sweeps amain,
And shrieks along the battle-plain:
The Chief, whose antique crownlet long
Still sparkled in the feudal song,
Now, from the mountain's misty throne,
Sees, in the thanedom once his own,
His ashes undistinguished lie,
His place, his power, his memory die:
His groans the lonely caverns fill,
His tears of rage impel the rill;
All mourn the minstrel's harp unstrung,
Their name unknown, their praise unsung.

III

Scarcely the hot assault was staid,
The terms of truce were scarcely made,
When they could spy, from Branksome's towers,
The advancing march of martial powers:

---

* In the original edition this appears as heae d due to a typesetting error.

Thick clouds of dust afar appeared,
And trampling steeds were faintly heard;
Bright spears, above the columns dun,
Glanced momentary to the sun;
And feudal banners fair displayed
The bands that moved to Branksome's aid.

IV

Vails not to tell each hardy clan,
    From the fair Middle Marches came;
The Bloody Heart blazed in the van,
    Announcing Douglas, dreaded name!
Vails not to tell what steeds did spurn,
Where the Seven Spears of Wedderburne
    Their men in battle-order set;
And Swinton laid the lance in rest,
That tamed of yore the sparkling crest
    Of Clarence's Plantagenet.
Nor list I say what hundreds more,
From the rich Merse and Lammermore,
And Tweed's fair borders, to the war,
Beneath the crest of old Dunbar,
    And Hepburn's mingled banners come,
Down the steep mountain glittering far,
    And shouting still, "a Home! a Home!"

V

Now squire and knight, from Branksome sent,
On many a courteous message went;

To every chief and lord they paid
Meet thanks for prompt and powerful aid;
And told them,—how a truce was made,
　　And how a day of fight was ta'en
　　'Twixt Musgrave and stout Deloraine;
　　　　And how the Ladye prayed them dear,
　　That all would stay the fight to see,
　　And deign, in love and courtesy,
　　　　To taste of Branksome cheer.
Nor, while they bade to feast each Scot,
Were England's noble Lords forgot;
Himself, the hoary Seneschal,
Rode forth, in seemly terms to call
Those gallant foes to Branksome Hall.
Accepted Howard, than whom knight
Was never dubbed, more bold in fight;
Nor, when from war and armour free,
More famed for stately courtesy:
But angry Dacre rather chose
In his pavilion to repose.

VI

Now, noble Dame, perchance you ask,
　　How these two hostile armies met?
Deeming it were no easy task
　　To keep the truce which here was set;
Where martial spirits, all on fire,
Breathed only blood and mortal ire.—
By mutual inroads, mutual blows,
By habit, and by nation, foes,

They met on Teviot's strand:
They met, and sate them mingled down,
Without a threat, without a frown,
　　As brothers meet in foreign land:
The hands, the spear that lately grasped,
Still in the mailed gauntlet clasped,
　　Were interchanged in greeting dear;
Visors were raised, and faces shewn,
And many a friend, to friend made known,
　　Partook of social cheer.
Some drove the jolly bowl about;
　　With dice and draughts some chased the day;
And some, with many a merry shout,
In riot, revelry, and rout,
　　Pursued the foot-ball play.

VII

Yet, be it known, had bugles blown,
　　Or sign of war been seen,
Those bands, so fair together ranged,
Those hands, so frankly interchanged,
　　Had dyed with gore the green:
The merry shout by Teviot-side
Had sunk in war-cries wild and wide,
　　And in the groan of death;
And whingers, * now in friendship bare,
The social meal to part and share,
　　Had found a bloody sheath.

* A sort of knife, or poniard.

'Twixt truce and war, such sudden change
Was not unfrequent, nor held strange,
    In the old Border-day;
But yet on Branksome's towers and town,
In peaceful merriment, sunk down
    The sun's declining ray.

VIII

The blithesome signs of wassel gay
Decayed not with the dying day;
Soon through the latticed windows tall,
Of lofty Branksome's lordly hall,
Divided square by shafts of stone,
Huge flakes of ruddy lustre shone;
Nor less the gilded rafters rang
With merry harp and beakers' clang;
    And frequent, on the darkening plain,
        Loud hollo, whoop, or whistle ran,
    As bands, their stragglers to regain,
        Give the shrill watch-word of their clan;
And revellers, o'er their bowls, proclaim
Douglas or Dacre's conquering name.

IX

Less frequent heard, and fainter still,
    At length the various clamours died;
And you might hear, from Branksome hill,
    No sound but Teviot's rushing tide;

Save, when the changing centinel
The challenge of his watch could tell;
And save, where, through the dark profound,
The clanging axe and hammer's sound
   Rung from the nether lawn;
For many a busy hand toiled there,
Strong pales to shape, and beams to square,
The lists' dread barriers to prepare,
   Against the morrow's dawn.

X

Margaret from hall did soon retreat,
   Despite the Dame's reproving eye;
Nor marked she, as she left her seat,
   Full many a stifled sigh:
For many a noble warrior strove
To win the Flower of Teviot's love,
   And many a bold ally.—
With throbbing head and anxious heart
All in her lonely bower apart,
   In broken sleep she lay:
By times, from silken couch she rose;
While yet the bannered hosts repose,
   She viewed the dawning day:
Of all the hundreds sunk to rest,
First woke the loveliest and the best.

XI

She gazed upon the inner court,
 Which in the tower's tall shadow lay;
Where coursers' clang, and stamp, and snort,
 Had rung the live-long yesterday;
Now still as death; till, stalking slow,—
 The jingling spurs announced his tread,—
A stately warrior passed below;
 But when he raised his plumed head—
  Blessed Mary! can it be?—
Secure, as if in Ousenam bowers,
He walks through Branksome's hostile towers,
 With fearless step and free.
She dared not sign, she dared not speak—
Oh! if one page's slumbers break,
 His blood the price must pay!
Not all the pearls Queen Mary wears,
Not Margaret's yet more precious tears,
 Shall buy his life a day.

XII

Yet was his hazard small; for well
You may bethink you of the spell
 Of that sly urchin Page;
This to his lord he did impart,
And made him seem, by glamour art,
 A knight from Hermitage.
Unchallenged, thus, the warder's post,
The court, unchallenged, thus he crossed,

For all the vassalage:
But, O! what magic's quaint disguise
Could blind fair Margaret's azure eyes!
    She started from her seat;
While with surprise and fear she strove,
And both could scarcely master love—
    Lord Henry's at her feet.

XIII

Oft have I mused, what purpose bad
That foul malicious urchin had
    To bring this meeting round;
For happy love's a heavenly sight,
And by a vile malignant sprite
    In such no joy is found:
And oft I've deemed, perchance he thought
Their erring passion might have wrought
    Sorrow, and sin, and shame;
And death to Cranstoun's gallant Knight,
And to the gentle Ladye bright,
    Disgrace, and loss of fame.
But earthly spirit could not tell
The heart of them that loved so well.
True love's the gift which God has given
To man alone beneath the heaven.
    It is not fantasy's hot fire,
        Whose wishes, soon as granted, fly;
    It liveth not in fierce desire,
        With dead desire it doth not die;

It is the secret sympathy,
The silver link, the silken tie,
Which heart to heart, and mind to mind,
In body and in soul can bind.—
Now leave we Margaret and her Knight,
To tell you of the approaching fight.

XIV

Their warning blast the bugles blew,
   The pipe's shrill port * aroused each clan;
In haste, the deadly strife to view,
   The trooping warriors eager ran:
Thick round the lists their lances stood,
Like blasted pines in Ettricke wood;
To Branksome many a look they threw,
The combatants' approach to view,
And bandied many a word of boast,
About the knight each favoured most.

XV

Meantime full anxious was the Dame;
For now arose disputed claim,
Of who should fight for Deloraine,
'Twixt Harden and 'twixt Thirlestaine:
   They 'gan to reckon kin and rent,
   And frowning brow on brow was bent;
     But yet not long the strife—for, lo!
   Himself, the Knight of Deloraine,
   Strong, as it seemed, and free from pain.
     In armour sheathed from top to toe,

---

*   A martial piece of music, adapted to the Bag-pipes.

Appeared, and craved the combat due.
The Dame her charm successful knew, *
And the fierce chiefs their claims withdrew.

XVI

When for the lists they sought the plain,
The stately Ladye's silken rein
   Did noble Howard hold;
Unarmed, by her side he walked,
And much, in courteous phrase, they talked
   Of feats of arms of old.
Costly his garb—his Flemish ruff
Fell o'er his doublet, shaped of buff,
   With satin slashed and lined;
Tawny his boot, and gold his spur,
His cloak was all of Poland fur,
   His hose with silver twined;
His Bilboa blade, by Marchmen felt,
Hung in a broad and studded belt;
Hence, in rude phrase, the Borderers still
Called noble Howard, Belted Will.

XVII

Behind Lord Howard and the Dame,
Fair Margaret on her palfrey came,
   Whose foot-cloth swept the ground;
White was her wimple, and her veil,
And her loose locks a chaplet pale
   Of whitest roses bound;

*   See p. 99. Stanza XXIII.

The lordly Angus, by her side,
In courtesy to cheer her tried;
Without his aid, her hand in vain
Had strove to guide her broidered rein.
He deemed, she shuddered at the sight
Of warriors met for mortal fight;
But cause of terror, all unguessed,
Was fluttering in her gentle breast,
When, in their chairs of crimson placed,
The Dame and she the barriers graced.

XVIII

Prize of the field, the young Buccleuch
An English knight led forth to view;
Scarce rued the boy his present plight,
So much he longed to see the fight.
Within the lists, in knightly pride,
High Home and haughty Dacre ride;
Their leading staffs of steel they wield,
As marshals of the mortal field;
While to each knight their care assigned
Like vantage of the sun and wind.
Then heralds hoarse did loud proclaim,
In king and queen, and wardens' name,
    That none, while lasts the strife,
Should dare, by look, or sign, or word,
Aid to a champion to afford,
    On peril of his life;
And not a breath the silence broke,
Till thus the alternate Heralds spoke:—

XIX

English herald

Here standeth Richard of Musgrave,
  Good knight and true, and freely born,
Amends from Deloraine to crave,
  For foul despiteous scathe and scorn.
He sayeth, that William of Deloraine
  Is traitor false by Border laws;
This with his sword he will maintain,
  So help him God, and his good cause!

XX

Scottish herald

Here standeth William of Deloraine,
Good knight and true, of noble strain,
Who sayeth, that foul treason's stain,
  Since he bore arms, ne'er soiled his coat;
    And that, so help him God above!
    He will on Musgrave's body prove,
  He lies most foully in his throat.

Lord Dacre

Forward, brave champions, to the fight!
Sound trumpets!——

Lord home

    ——"God defend the right!"
Then, Teviot! how thine echoes rang,
When bugle-sound and trumpet-clang

Let loose the martial foes,
And in mid list, with shield poised high,
And measured step and wary eye,
The combatants did close.

XXI

Ill would it suit your gentle ear,
Ye lovely listeners, to hear
How to the axe the helms did sound,
And blood poured down from many a wound;
For desperate was the strife, and long,
And either warrior fierce and strong.
But, were each dame a listening knight,
I well could tell how warriors fight;
For I have seen war's lightning flashing,
Seen the claymore with bayonet clashing,
Seen through red blood the war-horse dashing,
And scorned, amid the reeling strife,
To yield a step for death or life.

XXII

'Tis done, 'tis done! that fatal blow
Has stretched him on the bloody plain;
He strives to rise—Brave Musgrave, no!
Thence never shalt thou rise again!
He chokes in blood—some friendly hand
Undo the visor's barred band,
Unfix the gorget's iron clasp,
And give him room for life to gasp!—

O, bootless aid!—haste, holy Friar,
Haste, ere the sinner shall expire!
Of all his guilt let him be shriven,
And smooth his path from earth to heaven!

XXIII

In haste the holy Friar sped;—
His naked foot was dyed with red,
    As through the lists he ran;
Unmindful of the shouts on high,
That hailed the conqueror's victory,
    He raised the dying man;
Loose waved his silver beard and hair,
As o'er him he kneeled down in prayer;
And still the crucifix on high
He holds before his darkening eye;
And still he bends an anxious ear,
His faultering penitence to hear;
    Still props him from the bloody sod,
Still, even when soul and body part,
Pours ghostly comfort on his heart,
    And bids him trust in God!
Unheard he prays;—the death-pangs o'er!—
Richard of Musgrave breathes no more.

XXIV

As if exhausted in the fight,
Or musing o'er the piteous sight,

The silent victor stands;
His beaver did he not unclasp,
Marked not the shouts, felt not the grasp
  Of gratulating hands.
When lo! strange cries of wild surprise,
Mingled with seeming terror, rise
  Among the Scottish bands;
And all, amid the thronged array,
In panic haste gave open way
To a half-naked ghastly man,
Who downward from the castle ran:
He crossed the barriers at a bound,
  And wild and hagard looked around,
    As dizzy, and in pain;
  And all, upon the armed ground,
Knew William of Deloraine!
Each ladye sprung from seat with speed;
Vaulted each marshal from his steed;
  "And who art thou," they cried,
"Who hast this battle fought and won?"
His plumed helm was soon undone—
  "Cranstoun of Teviot-side!
For this fair prize I've fought and won,"—
And to the Ladye led her son.

XXV

Full oft the rescued boy she kissed,
And often pressed him to her breast;

For, under all her dauntless show,
Her heart had throbbed at every blow;
Yet not Lord Cranstoun deigned she greet,
Though low he kneeled at her feet.
Me lists not tell what words were made,
    What Douglas, Home, and Howard said—
—For Howard was a generous foe—
And how the clan united prayed,
    The Ladye would the feud forego,
And deign to bless the nuptial hour
Of Cranstoun's Lord and Teviot's Flower.

XXVI

She looked to river, looked to hill,
    Thought on the Spirit's prophecy,
Then broke her silence stern and still,—
    "Not you, but Fate, has vanquished me;
Their influence kindly stars may shower
On Teviot's tide and Branksome's tower,
    For pride is quelled, and love is free."—
She took fair Margaret by the hand,
Who, breathless, trembling, scarce might stand;
    That hand to Cranstoun's lord gave she:—
"As I am true to thee and thine,
Do thou be true to me and mine!
    This clasp of love our bond shall be;
For this is your betrothing day,
And all these noble lords shall stay,
    To grace it with their company."—

XXVII

All as they left the listed plain,
Much of the story she did gain;
How Cranstoun fought with Deloraine,
And of his Page, and of the Book,
Which from the wounded knight he took;
And how he sought her castle high,
That morn, by help of gramarye;
How, in Sir William's armour dight,
Stolen by his Page, while slept the knight,
He took on him the single fight.
But half his tale he left unsaid,
And lingered till he joined the maid.—
Cared not the Ladye to betray
Her mystic arts in view of day;
But well she thought, ere midnight came,
Of that strange Page the pride to tame,
From his foul hands the Book to save,
And send it back to Michael's grave.—
Needs not to tell each tender word
'Twixt Margaret and 'twixt Cranstoun's lord;
Nor how she told of former woes,
And how her bosom fell and rose,
While he and Musgrave bandied blows.—
Needs not these lovers' joys to tell;
One day, fair maids, you'll know them well.

XXVIII

William of Deloraine, some chance
Had wakened from his deathlike trancè;
   And taught that, in the listed plain,
Another, in his arms and shield,
Against fierce Musgrave axe did wield,
Under the name of Deloraine.
Hence, to the field, unarmed, he ran,
And hence his presence scared the clan,
Who held him for some fleeting wraith, *
And not a man of blood and breath.
   Not much this new ally he loved;
   Yet, when he saw what hap had proved,
      He greeted him right heartilie:
   He would not waken old debate,
   For he was void of rancorous hate,
      Though rude, and scant of courtesy;
In raids he spilt but seldom blood,
Unless when men at arms withstood,
Or, as was meet, for deadly feud.
He ne'er bore grudge for stalwart blow,
Ta'en in fair fight from gallant foe.
   And so 'twas seen of him, e'en now,
      When on dead Musgrave he looked down;
   Grief darkened on his rugged brow,
      Though halt disguised with a frown;
And thus, while sorrow bent his head,
His foeman's epitaph he made.

* The spectral apparition of a living person.

XXIX

"Now, Richard Musgrave, liest thou here!
　I ween, my deadly enemy;
For, if I slew thy brother dear,
　Thou slewest a sister's son to me:
And when I lay in dungeon dark,
　Of Naworth Castle, long months three,
Till ransomed for a thousand mark,
　Dark Musgrave, it was long of thee.
And, Musgrave, could our fight be tried,
　And thou wert now alive, as I,
No mortal man should us divide,
　Till one, or both of us, did die.
Yet rest thee God! for well I know,
I ne'er shall find a nobler foe.
In all the northern counties here,
Whose word is, Snafle, spur and spear, *
Thou wert the best to follow gear.
'Twas pleasure, as we looked behind,
To see how thou the chace couldst wind,
Cheer the dark blood-hound on his way,
And with the bugle rouse the fray!
I'd give the lands of Deloraine,
Dark Musgrave were alive again."—

---

* 　*The lands, that over Ouse to Berwick forth do bear,*
　Have for their blazon had, the snafle, spur, and spear,
　　　　　　　　　　Poly-albion, Song xiii

XXX

So mourned he, till Lord Dacre's band
Were bowning back to Cumberland.
They raised brave Musgrave from the field,
And laid him on his bloody shield;
On levelled lances, four and four,
By turns the noble burden bore.
Before, at times, upon the gale,
Was heard the Minstrel's plaintive wail;
Behind, four priests, in sable stole,
Sung requiem for the warrior's soul:
Around, the horsemen slowly rode;
With trailing pikes the spearmen trod;
And thus the gallant knight they bore,
Through Liddesdale, to Leven's shore;
Thence to Holme Coltrame's lofty nave,
And laid him in his father's grave.

———

THE harp's wild notes, though hushed the song,
The mimic march of death prolong;
Now seems it far, and now a-near,
Now meets, and now eludes the ear;
Now seems some mountain's side to sweep,
Now faintly dies in valley deep;
Seems now as if the Minstrel's wail,
Now the sad requiem, loads the gale;

Last, o'er the warrior's closing grave,
Rung the full choir in choral stave.

After due pause, they bade him tell,
Why he, who touched the harp so well,
Wander a poor and thankless soil,
Should thus, with ill-rewarded toil,
When the more generous southern land
Would well requite his skilful hand.

The Aged Harper, howsoe'er
His only friend, his harp, was dear,
Liked not to hear it ranked so high
Above his flowing poesy;
Less liked he still, that scornful jeer
Misprized the land, he loved so dear;
High was the sound, as thus again
The Bard resumed his minstrel strain.

THE

LAY OF THE LAST MINSTREL

CANTO SIXTH

―――――

I

BREATHES there the man, with soul so dead,
Who never to himself hath said,
   This is my own, my native land!
Whose heart hath ne'er within him burned,
As home his footsteps he hath turned,
   From wandering on a foreign strand!—
If such there breathe, go, mark him well;
For him no minstrel raptures swell
High though his titles, proud his name,
Boundless his wealth as wish can claim;
Despite those titles, power, and pelf,
The wretch, concentered all in self,
Living, shall forfeit fair renown,
And, doubly dying, shall go down
To the vile dust, from whence he sprung,
Unwept, unhonoured, and unsung.

II

O Caledonia! stern and wild,
Meet nurse for a poetic child!
Land of brown heath and shaggy wood,
Land of the mountain and the flood,
Land of my sires! what mortal hand
Can e'er untie the filial band,
That knits me to thy rugged strand!
Still, as I view each well-known scene,
Think what is now, and what hath been.
Seems as, to me, of all bereft,
Sole friends thy woods and streams were left
And thus I love them better still,
Even in extremity of ill.
By Yarrow's stream still let me stray,
Though none should guide my feeble way;
Still feel the breeze down Ettricke break,
Although it chill my withered cheek;
Still lay my head by Teviot-Stone,
Though there, forgotten and alone,
The Bard may draw his parting groan.

III

Not scorned like me! to Branksome Hall
The Minstrels came, at festive call;
Trooping they came, from near and far,
The jovial priests of mirth and war;
Alike for feast and fight prepared,
Battle and banquet both they shared.

Of late, before each martial clan,
They blew their death-note in the van,
But now, for every merry mate,
Rose the portcullis' iron grate;
They sound the pipe, they strike the string,
They dance, they revel, and they sing,
Till the rude turrets shake and ring.

IV

Me lists not at this tide declare
   The splendour of the spousal rite,
How mustered in the chapel fair
   Both maid and matron, squire and knight;
Me lists not tell of owches rare,
Of mantles green, and braided hair,
And kirtles furred with miniver;
What plumage waved the altar round,
How spurs, and ringing chainlets, sound:
And hard it were for bard to speak
The changeful hue of Margaret's cheek;
That lovely hue which comes and flies,
As awe and shame alternate rise!

V

Some bards have sung, the Ladye high
Chapel or altar came not nigh;
Nor durst the rites of spousal grace,
So much she feared each holy place.
False slanders these:—I trust right well,
She wrought not by forbidden spell;

For mighty words and signs have power
O'er sprites in planetary hour:
Yet scarce I praise their venturous part,
Who tamper with such dangerous art.
    But this for faithful truth I say,—
        The Ladye by the altar stood,
    Of sable velvet her array,
        And on her head a crimson hood,
With pearls embroidered and entwined,
Guarded with gold, with ermine lined;
A merlin sat upon her wrist,
Held by a leash of silken twist.

VI

The spousal rites were ended soon:
'Twas now the merry hour of noon,
And in the lofty arched hall
Was spread the gorgeous festival.
Steward and squire, with heedful haste,
Marshalled the rank of every guest;
Pages, with ready blade, were there,
The mighty meal to carve and share:
O'er capon, heron-shew, and crane,
And princely peacock's gilded train,
And o'er the boar-head, garnished brave,
And cygnet from St Mary's wave;
O'er ptarmigan and venison,
The priest had spoke his benison.
Then rose the riot and the din,
Above, beneath, without, within!

For, from the lofty balcony,
Rung trumpet, shalm, and psaltery;
Their clanging bowls old warriors quaffed,
Loudly they spoke, and loudly laughed;
Whispered young knights, in tone more mild,
To ladies fair, and ladies smiled.
The hooded hawks, high perched on beam,
The clamour joined with whistling scream,
And napped their wings, and shook their bells,
In concert with the staghounds' yells.
Round go the flasks of ruddy wine,
From Bourdeaux, Orleans, or the Rhine;
Their tasks the busy sewers ply,
And all is mirth and revelry.

VII

The Goblin Page, omitting still
No opportunity of ill,
Strove now, while blood ran hot and high,
To rouse debate and jealousy;
Till Conrad, lord of Wolfenstein,
By nature fierce, and warm with wine,
And now in humour highly crossed,
About some steeds his band had lost,
High words to words succeeding still,
Smote, with his gauntlet, stout Hunthill;
A hot and hardy Rutherford,
Whom men call Dickon Draw-the-Sword.

He took it on the Page's saye,
Hunthill had driven these steeds away.
Then Howard, Home, and Douglas rose,
The kindling discord to compose:
Stern Rutherford right little said,
But bit his glove, and shook his head.—
A fortnight thence, in Inglewood,
Stout Conrad, cold, and drenched in blood,
His bosom gored with many a wound,
Was by a woodman's lyme-dog found;
Unknown the manner of his death,
Gone was his brand, both sword and sheath;
But ever from that time, 'twas said,
That Dickon wore a Cologne blade.

VIII

The Dwarf, who feared his master's eye
Might his foul treachery espie,
Now sought the castle buttery,
Where many a yeoman, bold and free,
Revelled as merrily and well
As those, that sat in lordly selle.
Watt Tinlinn, there, did frankly raise
The pledge to Arthur Fire-the-Braes;
And he, as by his breeding bound,
To Howard's merry-men sent it round.
To quit them, on the English side,
Red Roland Forster loudly cried,
"A deep carouse to yon fair bride!"

At every pledge, from vat and pail,
Foamed forth, in floods, the nut-brown ale;
While shout the riders every one,
Such day of mirth ne'er cheered their clan,
Since old Buccleuch the name did gain,
When in the cleuch the buck was ta'en.

IX

The wily Page, with vengeful thought,
    Remembered him of Tinlinn's yew,
And swore, it should be dearly bought,
    That ever he the arrow drew.
First, he the yeoman did molest,
With bitter gibe and taunting jest;
Told, how he fled at Solway strife,
And how Hob Armstrong cheered his wife.
Then, shunning still his powerful arm,
At unawares he wrought him harm;
From trencher stole his choicest cheer,
Dashed from his lips his can of beer,
Then, to his knee sly creeping on,
With bodkin pierced him to the bone:
The venomed wound, and festering joint,
Long after rued that bodkin's point.
The startled yeoman swore and spurned,
And board and flaggons overturned.
Riot and clamour wild began;
Back to the hall the Urchin ran;
Took in a darkling nook his post,
And grinned, and muttered, "Lost! lost! lost!"

X

By this, the Dame, lest further fray
Should mar the concord of the day,
Had bid the Minstrels tune their lay.
And first stept forth old Albert Graeme,
The Minstrel of that ancient name:
Was none who struck the harp so well,
Within the Land Debateable;
Well friended too, his hardy kin,
Whoever lost, were sure to win;
They sought the beeves, that made their broth,
In Scotland and in England both.
In homely guise, as nature bade,
His simple song the Borderer said.

XI

ALBERT GRAEME

It was an English ladye bright,
    (The sun shines fair on Carlisle wall,)
And she would marry a Scottish knight,
    For Love will still be lord of all.

Blithely they saw the rising sun,
    When he shone fair on Carlisle wall,
But they were sad ere day was done,
    Though Love was still the lord of all.

Her sire gave brooch and jewel fine,
    Where the sun shines fair on Carlisle wall;
Her brother gave but a flask of wine,
    For ire that Love was lord of all.

For she had lands, both meadow and lea,
    Where the sun shines fair on Carlisle wall,
And he swore her death, ere he would see
    A Scottish knight the lord of all.

XII

That wine she had not tasted well,
    (The sun shines fair on Carlisle wall;)
When dead, in her true love's arms, she fell,
    For Love was still the lord of all.

He pierced her brother to the heart,
    Where the sun shines fair on Carlisle wall;—
So perish all, would true love part,
    That Love may still be lord of all!

And then he took the Cross divine,
    Where the sun shines fair on Carlisle wall,
And died for her sake in Palestine,
    So Love was still the lord of all.

Now all ye lovers, that faithful prove,
    (The sun shines fair on Carlisle wall,)
Pray for their souls, who died for love,
    For Love shall still be lord of all!

XIII

As ended Albert's simple lay,
    Arose a Bard of loftier port;
For sonnet, rhyme, and roundelay,
    Renowned in haughty Henry's court:
There rung thy harp, unrivalled long,
Fitztraver, of the silver song!
    The gentle Surrey loved his lyre—
      Who has not heard of Surrey's fame?
    His was the hero's soul of fire,
      And his the bard's immortal name,
And his was love, exalted high
By all the glow of chivalry.

XIV

They sought, together, climes afar,
    And oft, within some olive grove,
When evening came, with twinkling star,
    They sung of Surrey's absent love.
His step the Italian peasant staid,
    And deemed that spirits from on high,
Round where some hermit saint was laid,
    Were breathing heavenly melody;
So sweet did harp and voice combine,
To praise the name of Geraldine.

XV

Fitztraver! O what tongue may say
   The pangs thy faithful bosom knew,
When Surrey, of the deathless lay,
   Ungrateful Tudor's sentence slew!
Regardless of the tyrant's frown,
His harp called wrath and vengeance down.
He left, for Naworth's iron towers,
Windsor's green glades, and courtly bowers,
And, faithful to his patron's name,
With Howard still Fitztraver came;
Lord William's foremost favourite he,
And chief of all his minstrelsy.

XVI

Fitztraver

'Twas All-souls eve, and Surrey's heart beat high;
   He heard the midnight-bell with anxious start,
Which told the mystic hour, approaching nigh,
   When wise Cornelius promised, by his art,
To shew to him the ladye of his heart,
   Albeit betwixt them roared the ocean grim;
Yet so the sage had hight to play his part,
   That he should see her form in life and limb,
And mark, if still she loved, and still she thought
     of him.

XVII

Dark was the vaulted room of gramarye,
   To which the Wizard led the gallant Knight,
Save that before a mirror, huge and high,
   A hallowed taper shed a glimmering light
On mystic implements of magic might;
   On cross, and character, and talisman,
And almagest, and altar, nothing bright:
   For fitful was the lustre, pale and wan,
As watch-light by the bed of some departing man.

XVIII

But soon, within that mirror, huge and high,
   Was seen a self-emitted light to gleam;
And forms upon its breast the earl 'gan spy,
   Cloudy and indistinct, as feverish dream;
Till, slow arranging, and defined, they seem
   To form a lordly and a lofty room,
Part lighted by a lamp with silver beam,
   Placed by a couch of Agra's silken loom,
And part by moonshine pale, and part was hid in
     gloom.

XIX

Fair all the pageant—but how passing fair
   The slender form, which lay on couch of Ind!
O'er her white bosom strayed her hazel hair,
   Pale her dear cheek, as if for love she pined;
All in-her night-robe loose, she lay reclined,

And, pensive, read from tablet eburnine
Some strain, that seemed her inmost soul to find:—
That favoured strain was Surrey's raptured line,
That fair and lovely form, the Ladye Geraldine.

XX

Slow rolled the clouds upon the lovely form,
    And swept the goodly vision all away—
So royal envy rolled the murky storm
    O'er my beloved Master's glorious day.
Thou jealous, ruthless tyrant! Heaven repay
    On thee, and on thy childrens' latest line,
The wild caprice of thy despotic sway,
    The gory bridal bed, the plundered shrine,
The murdered Surrey's blood, the tears of Geraldine!

XXI

Both Scots, and Southern chiefs, prolong
Applauses of Fitztraver's song:

These hated Henry's name as death,
And those still held the ancient faith.—
Then, from his seat, with lofty air,
Rose Harold, bard of brave St Clair;
St Clair, who, feasting high at Home,
Had with that lord to battle come.
Harold was born where restless seas
Howl round the storm-swept Orcades;
Where erst St Clairs held princely sway
O'er isle and islet, strait and bay;—

Still nods their palace to its fall,
Thy pride and sorrow, fair Kirkwall!—
Thence oft he marked fierce Pentland rave,
As if grim Odinn rode her wave;
And watched, the whilst, with visage pale,
And throbbing heart, the struggling sail;
For all of wonderful and wild
Had rapture for the lonely child.

XXII

And much of wild and wonderful
In these rude isles might Fancy cull;
For thither came, in times afar,
Stern Lochlin's sons of roving war,
The Norsemen, trained to spoil and blood,
Skilled to prepare the raven's food;
Kings of the main their leaders brave,
Their barks the dragons of the wave.
And there, in many a stormy vale,
The Scald had told his wond'rous tale;
And many a Runic column high
Had witnessed grim idolatry.
And thus had Harold, in his youth,
Learned many a Saga's rhyme uncouth,—
Of that Sea-Snake, tremendous curled,
Whose monstrous circle girds the world;
Of those dread Maids, whose hideous yell
Maddens the battle's bloody swell;

Of chiefs, who, guided through the gloom
By the pale death-lights of the tomb,
Ransacked the graves of warriors old,
Their faulchions wrenched from corpses' hold,
Waked the deaf tomb with war's alarms,
And bade the dead arise to arms!
With war and wonder all on flame,
To Roslin's bowers young Harold came,
Where, by sweet glen and greenwood tree,
He learned a milder minstrelsy;
Yet something of the Northern spell
Mixed with the softer numbers well.

XXIII

HAROLD

O listen, listen, ladies gay!
　　No haughty feat of arms I tell:
Soft is the note, and sad the lay,
　　That mourns the lovely Rosabelle.
　—"Moor, moor the barge, ye gallant crew!
　　And, gentle ladye, deign to stay!
Rest thee in Castle Ravensheuch,
　　Nor tempt the stormy firth to-day.

"The blackening wave is edged with white;
　　To inch * and rock the sea-mews fly;
The fishers have heard the Water Sprite,
　　Whose screams forebode that wreck is nigh.

*　　*Inch* Isle

"Last night the gifted Seer did view
    A wet shroud swathed round ladye gay;
Then stay thee, Fair, in Ravensheuch:
Why cross the gloomy firth today?"—
" 'Tis not because Lord Lindesay's heir
    To-night at Roslin leads the ball,
But that my ladye-mother there
    Sits lonely in her castle-hall.

" 'Tis not because the ring they ride,
    And Lindesay at the ring rides well,
But that my sire the wine will chide,
    If 'tis not filled by Rosabelle."—

O'er Roslin all that dreary night
    A wondrous blaze was seen to gleam;
'Twas broader than the watch-fire light,
    And redder than the bright moon-beam.

It glared on Roslin s castled rock,
    It ruddied all the copse-wood glen;
'Twas seen from Dreyden's groves of oak,
    And seen from caverned Hawthornden.

Seemed all on fire that chapel proud.
    Where Roslin's chiefs uncoffined lie;
Each Baron, for a sable shroud,
    Sheathed in his iron panoply.

Seemed all on fire within, around,
    Deep sacristy and altar's pale;
Shone every pillar foliage-bound,
    And glimmered all the dead men's mail.

Blazed battlement and pinnet high,
    Blazed every rose-carved buttress fair—
So still they blaze, when fate is nigh
    The lordly line of high St Clair.

There are twenty of Roslin's barons bold
    Lie buried within that proud chapelle;
Each one the holy vault doth hold—
    But the sea holds lovely Rosabelle!

And each St Clair was buried there,
    With candle, with book, and with knell;
But the sea-caves rung, and the wild winds sung,
    The dirge of lovely Rosabelle.

XXV

So sweet was Harold's piteous lay,
    Scarce marked the guests the darkened hall,
Though, long before the sinking day,
    A wondrous shade involved them all:
It was not eddying mist or fog,
Drained by the sun from fen or bog;
    Of no eclipse had sages told;
And yet, as it came on apace,
Each one could scarce his neighbour's face,
    Could scarce his own stretched hand behold.

A secret horror checked the feast,
And chilled the soul of every guest;
Even the high Dame stood half aghast,
She knew some evil on the blast;
The elvish Page fell to the ground,
And, shuddering, muttered, "Found! found!
    found!"

XXVI

Then sudden, through the darkened air
    A flash of lightning came;
So broad, so bright, so red the glare,
    The castle seemed on flame;
Glanced every rafter of the hall,
Glanced every shield upon the wall;
Each trophiecl beam, each sculptured stone,
Were instant seen, and instant gone;
Full through the guests' bedazzled band
Resistless flashed the levin-brand,
And filled the hall with smouldering smoke,
As on the elvish Page it broke.
    It broke, with thunder long and loud,
    Dismayed the brave, appalled the proud,—
        From sea to sea the larum rung;
    On Berwick wall, and at Carlisle withal,
        To arms the startled warders sprung.
When ended was the dreadful roar,
The elvish Dwarf was seen no more!

XXVII

Some heard a voice in Branksome Hall,
Some saw a sight, not seen by all;
That dreadful voice was heard by some,
Cry, with loud summons, "GYLBIN, COME!"
   And on the spot where burst the brand,
     Just where the Page had flung him down,
   Some saw an arm, and some a hand,
     And some the waving of a gown.
The guests in silence prayed and shook,
And terror dimmed each lofty look.
But none of all the astonished train
Was so dismayed as Deloraine;
His blood did freeze, his brain did burn,
'Twas feared his mind would ne'er return;
   For he was speechless, ghastly, wan,
   Like him, of whom the story ran,
   Who spoke the spectre-hound in Man. *
     At length, by fits, he darkly told,
     With broken hint, and shuddering cold—
   That he had seen, right certainly,
A shape with amice wrapped around.
With a wrought Spanish baldric bound,
   Like pilgrim from beyond the sea;
And knew—but how it mattered not—
It was the wizard, Michael Scott.

---

* The Isle of Man.

XXVIII

The anxious crowd, with horror pale,
All trembling, heard the wondrous tale;
   No sound was made, no word was spoke,
   Till noble Angus silence broke;
     And he a solemn sacred plight
    Did to St Bride of Douglas make,
    That he a pilgrimage would take
    To Melrose Abbey, for the sake
     Of Michael's restless sprite.
Then each, to ease his troubled breast,
To some blessed saint his prayers addressed:
Some to St Modan made their vows,
Some to St Mary of the Lowes,
Some to the Holy Rood of Lisle,
Some to Our Lady of the Isle;
Each did his patron witness make,
That he such pilgrimage would take,
And Monks should sing, and bells should toll,
All for the weal of Michael's soul.
While vows were ta'en, and prayers were prayed,
'Tis said the noble Dame, dismayed,
Renounced, for aye, dark magic's aid.

XXIX

Nought of the bridal will I tell,
Which after in short space befel;
Nor how brave sons and daughters fair
Blessed Teviot's Flower, and Cranstoun's heir:

After such dreadful scene, 'twere vain
To wake the note of mirth again.
More meet it were to mark the day
   Of penitence and prayer divine,
When pilgrim-chiefs, in sad array,
   Sought Melrose' holy shrine.

XXX

With naked foot, and sackcloth vest,
And arms enfolded on his breast,
   Did every pilgrim go;
The standers-by might hear uneath,
Footstep, or voice, or high-drawn breath,
   Through all the lengthened row:
No lordly look, nor martial stride,
Gone was their glory, sunk their pride,
   Forgotten their renown;
Silent and slow, like ghosts, they glide
To the high altar's hallowed side,
   And there they kneeled them down:
Above the suppliant chieftains wave
The banners of departed brave;
Beneath the lettered stones were laid
The ashes of their fathers dead:
From many a garnished niche around,
Stern saints, and tortured martyrs, frowned.

XXXI

And slow up the dim aisle afar,
With sable cowl and scapular,
And snow-white stoles, in order due,
The holy Fathers, two and two,
    In long procession came;
Taper, and host, and book they bare,
And holy banner, flourished fair
    With the Redeemer's name:
Above the prostrate pilgrim band
The mitred Abbot stretched his hand,
    And blessed them as they kneeled;
With holy cross he signed them all,
And prayed they might be sage in hall,
    And fortunate in field.
Then mass was sung, and prayers were said,
And solemn requiem for the dead;
And bells tolled out their mighty peal,
For the departed spirit's weal;
And ever in the office close
The hymn of intercession rose;
And far the echoing aisles prolong
The awful burthen of the song,—
        DIES IRAE, DIES ILLA,
        SOLVET SAECLUM IN FAVILLA
While the pealing organ rung;
    Were it meet with sacred strain
    To close my lay, so light and vain,
Thus the holy Fathers sung.

XXXII

Hymn for the Dead

That day of wrath, that dreadful day,
When heaven and earth shall pass away,
What power shall be the sinner's stay!
How shall he meet that dreadful day,
When, shrivelling like a parched scroll,
The flaming heavens together roll;
When louder yet, and yet more dread,
Swells the high trump that wakes the dead!

O! on that day, that wrathful day,
When man to judgment wakes from clay,
Be Thou the trembling sinner's stay,
Though heaven and earth shall pass away!

———

Hushed is the harp—the Minstrel gone.
And did he wander forth alone?
Alone, in indigence and age,
To linger out his pilgrimage?
No:—close beneath proud Newark's tower,
Arose the Minstrel's lowly bower;
A simple hut; but there was seen
The little garden hedged with green,
The cheerful hearth, and lattice clean.
There sheltered wanderers, by the blaze,
Oft heard the tale of other days;

For much he loved to ope his door,
And give the aid he begged before.
So passed the winter's day; but still,
When summer smiled on sweet Bowhill,
And July's eve, with balmy breath,
Waved the blue-bells on Newark heath;
When throstles sung in Hare-head shaw,
And corn was green on Carterhaugh,
And flourished, broad, Blackandro's oak,
The aged Harper's soul awoke!
Then would he sing achievements high,
And circumstance of chivalry,
Till the rapt traveller would stay,
Forgetful of the closing day;
And noble youths, the strain to hear,
Forsook the hunting of the deer,
And Yarrow, as he rolled along,
Bore burden to the Minstrel's song.